Blenko

1972-1983 Catalogs

Leslie Piña

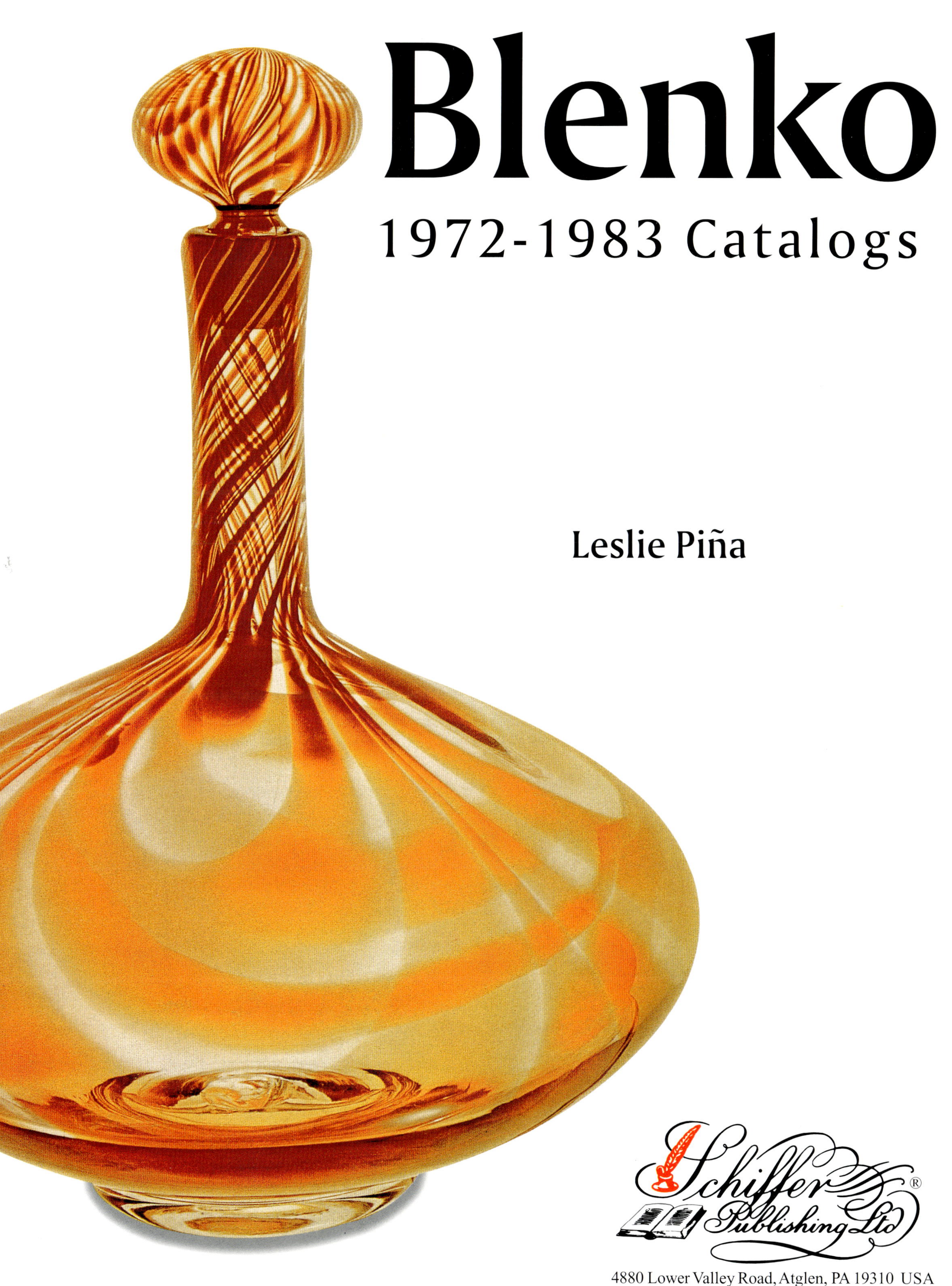

Schiffer Publishing Ltd®

4880 Lower Valley Road, Atglen, PA 19310 USA

Acknowledgments

Many thanks to Richard Blenko for lending company catalogs and to Rosalind Young at the Rakow Library at the Corning Glass Museum for assistance researching the designers. Thanks to Doug Congdon-Martin and to Ramón for helping with the photography and to the staff at Schiffer Publishing for all that they do.

Library of Congress Card Number: 00-111900

Designed by Leslie Piña
Layout by Bonnie M. Hensley
Type set in CopprplGoth Bd BT/Korinna BT

ISBN: 0-7643-1383-5
Printed in China
1 2 3 4

Published by Schiffer Publishing Ltd.
4880 Lower Valley Road
Atglen, PA 19310
Phone: (610) 593-1777; Fax: (610) 593-2002
E-mail: Schifferbk@aol.com
Please visit our web site catalog at **www.schifferbooks.com**

In Europe, Schiffer books are distributed by Bushwood Books
6 Marksbury Avenue Kew Gardens
Surrey TW9 4JF England
Phone: 44 (0) 20-8392-8585; Fax: 44 (0) 20-8392-9876
E-mail: Bushwd@aol.com
Free postage in the UK. Europe: air mail at cost.

This book may be purchased from the publisher.
Include $3.95 for shipping. Please try your bookstore first.
We are always looking for people to write books on new and related subjects.
If you have an idea for a book please contact us at the above address.
You may write for a free catalog.

Contents

Chronology

1854 William John Blenko born in London, England.

1893 Blenko goes to America, arrives in Kokomo, Indiana to begin making stained glass; finds himself in the midst of an economic depression with 20% unemployment and no churches to use his stained glass.

1897 William Henry Blenko is born in Kokomo.

1903 After the Kokomo factory fails, Blenko returns to England with his family.

1909 Tries again in America, this time in Point Marion, Pennsylvania.

1911 After another failure, Blenko begins making glass in Clarksburg, West Virginia.

1913 Blenko gives up.

1920 William Henry Blenko marries Marian Hunt, daughter of a Pittsburgh glass designer.

1921 Blenko recovers from past failures and begins in Milton, West Virginia. He calls the company Eureka Art Glass Co., because he discovered the valuable formula for ruby glass and shouted, "Eureka, I found it!"

1922 Blenko's son William Henry (Bill) joins his glass business.

1929 Experiments making decorative tableware for Carbones of Boston.

1930s No market for stained glass during the Depression, so Bill Blenko begins to focus on tableware. He hires Swedish glassmakers from the Huntington Tumbler Co., Axil (glassblower) and Louis (finisher) Muller to teach workers how to make quality table and decorative ware for Blenko.

1932 Macy's in New York begins to carry Blenko tableware.

1933 William John Blenko dies, leaving Bill as president; Blenko glass is featured at the "Century of Progress" Chicago World's Fair.

1936 Colonial Williamsburg contracts Blenko to make their glass reproductions.

late 1930s

Carl Ebert Erickson (1899-1966) works at Blenko; he and his brother head Erickson Glassworks in Bremen, Ohio 1943-1961.

early 1940s

World War II, 41 glassworkers drafted, Bill Blenko is a captain in the Air Corps, production halted.

1946 New factory built, booming postwar economy creates new demand for both stained glass and tableware.

1946 Winslow Anderson begins as the first design director and elevates the level of artistic achievement.

1952 Wayne Husted begins as the second design director and introduces oversized stoppered bottles and other fifties icons.

1959 First all-color catalog created by Husted, who also designs the new sandblasted Blenko signature used on glass.

1960 Only other year to use sandblasted signature.

1960s Glass artists and members of the new studio glass movement come to Blenko to learn.

1963 Joel Myers begins as design director and also learns to blow glass.

1966 Blenko Visitors' Center opens; Colonial Williamsburg reproductions discontinued.

1969 Bill Blenko dies, leaving his son William Henry, Jr., as president; many West Virginia glass companies are forced to close because of foreign competition and increased production costs.

1970 John Nickerson begins as design director.

1975 Don Shepherd begins as design director.

1980 First West Virginia Annual Birthday Piece, by Don Shepherd.

1987 Publication of *Blenko Glass 1930-1953.*

1988 Hank Adams begins as design director.

1994 Chris Gibbons begins as design director.

1995 Matthew Carter begins as design director.

1996 William Blenko steps down, and Richard Deakin Blenko becomes president.

1998 Documentary on Blenko's history, *Hearts of Glass,* first aired on public television.

1999 Huntington Museum of Art holds special exhibit to honor Blenko and its first design director, Winslow Anderson.

Introduction

Foil hand label used until 1982.

Large B label shown in 1983 catalog.

This reprint of the 1972-1983 Blenko catalogs is the third in the trilogy on Blenko Glass from the early and "middle" years. The year 1983 marks the beginning of the "late" period when the label was changed from the silver foil hand to the square with large B and red dot. The early years of the 1940s through the 1960s are the most popular with collectors of Blenko Glass. However, interest in the 1970s is awakening, and some items from the 1970s are already commanding high prices in the secondary markets both on-line and "in person."

John Nickerson and Don Shepherd were the two staff designers responsible for all of the newly-introduced glass in the following catalogs. Many of their designs were inspired by those of their predecessors — those great designers of "cool 50s and 60s glass" — Winslow Anderson, Wayne Husted, and Joel Myers. For the sake of economy, designers were encouraged to utilize many of the older molds as a starting point for new introductions. Other 1970s designs are original and on their way to becoming classics from this slightly later period.

John Henry Nickerson

Born May 15, 1939 in Minneapolis, Nickerson earned a Bachelor of Science degree from Montana State University in Bozeman, Montana, in 1964, and a Masters of Fine Arts from the New York State College of Ceramics, Alfred University in Alfred, New York, in 1969. He also studied at the Society of Arts and Crafts in Detroit, Michigan and the School for American Craftsmen, Rochester Institute of Technology. His work has been exhibited both nationally and internationally and was included in the important catalog *New Glass: A Worldwide Survey* by the Corning Glass Museum in 1979. He joined Blenko Glass as design director in 1970 and stayed until 1975.

#7222-X Charisma bottle/decanter and #7239-X Charisma tall bottle, designed by John Nickerson and produced only in 1972. 21" h.

#7223 tall bottle-vase in Turquoise (Blenko Blue), designed by Nickerson. 25"h.

Top left: #7323 and #7412 decanters in Tangerine, by Nickerson. 13" and 11"h.

Bottom left: #7328 jar with large mushroom lid, by Nickerson for 1973. 12" h.

Bottom right: #7515L bottle with applied medallion, by Nickerson for 1975. 10" h.

Donald A. Shepherd

Born October 9, 1930, Shepherd studied at the California School of Fine Arts and at the Catan-Rose Institute of Fine Arts in New York from 1953 to 1957. His work has been exhibited both nationally and internationally and was also included in the *New Glass: A Worldwide Survey* catalog.

After graduating from art school he joined one of his professors to form a studio in New York City specializing in stained glass. In 1959 he first became acquainted with Blenko when he went to the factory to purchase stained glass. In 1969/1970 he designed a variety of metal molds for a line of free form vessels that could be produced by a factory. A line of 24 vases and bottles were made at the Chalet Glass Factory in Cornwall, Canada, in 1970 and were marketed for about three years under the trade name *Glass America.* Shepherd joined Blenko in 1975 and stayed as their design director until 1988.

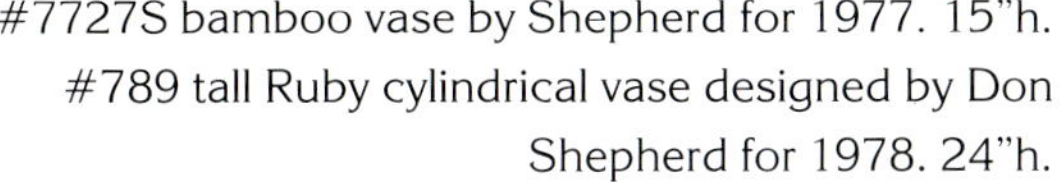

#7727S bamboo vase by Shepherd for 1977. 15"h. #789 tall Ruby cylindrical vase designed by Don Shepherd for 1978. 24"h.

#828 Balloons in Crystal with Lemon and Honey with Tangerine, designed by Shepherd for 1982. 11"h.

#7929 Toad vase in Wheat, by Shepherd. 10-1/2"h.

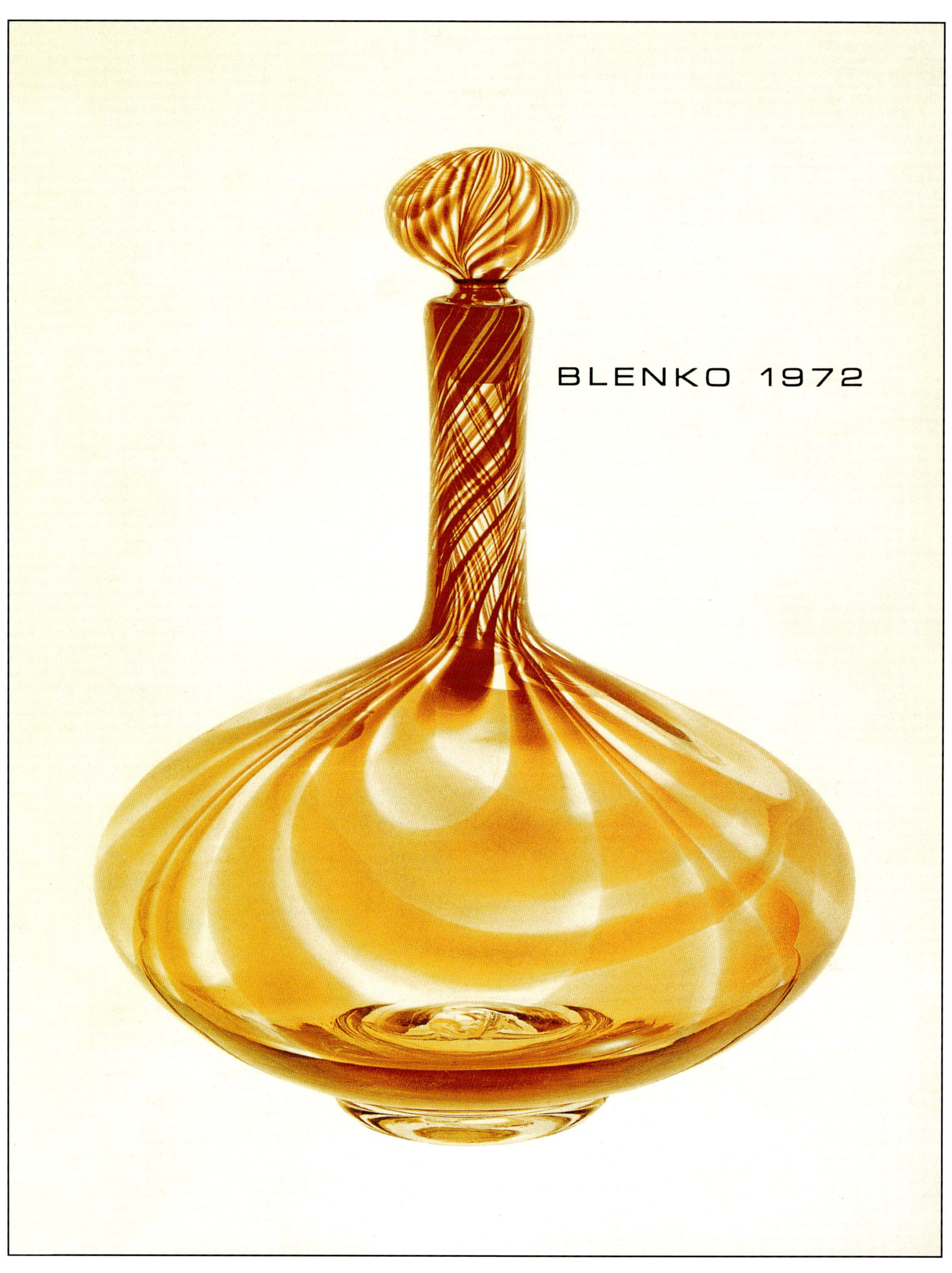
BLENKO 1972

BLENKO COLORS 1972

† NUMBERS PRECEDED BY A DAGGER ARE NOT AVAILABLE IN TANGERINE.
* NUMBERS PRECEDED BY AN ASTERISK ARE AVAILABLE IN CRACKLED AS WELL AS PLAIN FINISH.
EACH PIECE IS AVAILABLE IN SIX COLORS, UNLESS MARKED OTHERWISE.
CHARISMA ITEMS SOLD ONLY AS SHOWN ON PAGE 15.

7112
14" high
$10.50
7213
15¾" high
$10.00
*7215L
11" high
$9.00
*7215S
8" high
$6.00
7120
12½" high
$8.00
7017
7¼" high
$4.50
7222
20¾" high
$12.50
6937
22¼" high approx.
$10.50
7127
13" high
$12.00
7118
21½" high
$10.50
*729
11¾" high
$7.50
*727
8½" high
$6.50
†990A
3⅛" dia.
$1.00 ea.
*990
12" high
$8.00
Shade only
7048
19½" high
$18.00

*7111
12″ high
$7.50
*722M
8″ high
$6.00
*722L
9½″ high
$7.00
*722S
6½″ high
$5.00
*7224
15½″ high
$10.00
*7228S
6½″ high
$6.50
*7228L
8½″ high
$7.50
*7228M
7½″ high
$7.00
*7228LL
9½″ high
$8.00
6212
20½″ high
$12.00
7119W/S
18″ high
$12.00
Crystal stopper with tangerine and emerald bottles
7119
14½″ high
$8.00
7114
16½″ high
$12.50
*7126
14″ high
$10.00
6741
23¼″ high
$16.00
Crystal stopper with tangerine and emerald bottles

971L
22″ long
$31.50

971M
16″ long
$16.00

5433
10″ high
$14.00

*67S
15″ high
6¾″ dia. at base
$14.00
Crystal only

7231
9½″ dia.
$10.00

6918
Discontinued

*728
7¾″ high
$6.50

*719
17″ high
$8.00

*7121
10½″ high
$8.50

715
8″ high
$6.00

6914
8″ high
$5.00

6916
6½″ high
$6.50

6919
9½″ high
$6.50

*629
8½" high
$9.00

*629S
6" high
$7.50

*7227M
10¼" high
$7.50

*7227L
12½" high
$8.50

*7227S
8" high
$6.50

6716
14¼" high
$16.00
No tangerine or emerald stoppers

7226S
11½" high
$9.00

7226L
21½" high
$25.00

7226M
16" high
$12.00

7221
17¾" high
$10.00

7051
21⅝" high
$13.00

No tangerine or
emerald stoppers
7029
16½" high
$9.50
6953
21" high
$15.00
7219
16¼" high
$9.00
6810
10¾" high
$6.00
6811
16¼" high
$9.00
6952
13" high
$10.50
6955
22¾" high
$18.00
7223
25" high approx.
$10.00
7218
11¼" high
$8.50
706
6¾" high
$4.00
709
6¾" high
$5.50
7049
22" high
$15.00
6954
27¼" high
$15.00

6934
20½" high
$12.00
No tangerine or
emerald stoppers
7220L
15¾" high
$9.00
7220S
13" high
$7.50
6956
21" high
$13.50
7033
16⅜" high
$10.00
*7211
8½" high
$6.50
6935
13½" high
$8.50
*7166L
13" high
$7.50
*7166M
10" high
$6.00
*726
7" high
$5.50
6942
11⅝" high
$8.00
6928
20¼" high
$10.00
991
13½" high
$8.00
6951
24" high
$13.50

6511 9½" high $6.00
°3750L 5½" high $5.50
721 5½" high $3.00
°7217L 8¾" high $12.00
°7217S 6½" high $10.00
°6714 9¾" high $8.50
°418S 4½" high $2.00
°418L 6" high $2.00
°6516 14½" high $8.50
°636S 8" high $6.00
717 15" high $7.50
°7214S 8" high $6.00
°7214L 11" high $9.00
°6424 5" high $3.00
°708 7 9/16" high $4.00
7141 9" high $5.50
°6944 9½" high $6.50
°7210 8" high $8.50
64D 11" high $3.00
°705 6⅛" high $3.00
°64B 11" high $3.00
°7018 13⅜" high $7.00
°7216 13" high $9.00
°7117 8" high $6.50
°713 10½" high $4.50
707 6⅛" high $4.00

51S
bubbles only
3" dia.
$9.00 doz.
51L
bubbles only
6" dia.
$24.00 doz.
51M
bubbles only
4½" dia.
$15.60 doz.
*6840
6" high
15½" dia.
$12.00
*7028
5" high
11" dia.
$7.50
*6950
7¾" high
$10.00
*3744X
7" dia.
$4.00
*37
13" high
$8.00
*49
10½" high
$8.00
384
7½" high
$3.50
*7212
11½" high
$9.00
724
4½" high
$4.00
723
4½" high
$4.00
*388
7½" high
$7.50
6320
3¼" dia.
$6.00
59
Mixed colors only
$1.00 box
472
$1.50 box
†699B
6½" high
$6.50 pr.
†699A
6½" high
$6.50 pr.
†6813
7" high
$6.50 pr.
†6725
3½" high
3¾" wide
$6.50 pr.
†434
5½" high
$6.50 pr.

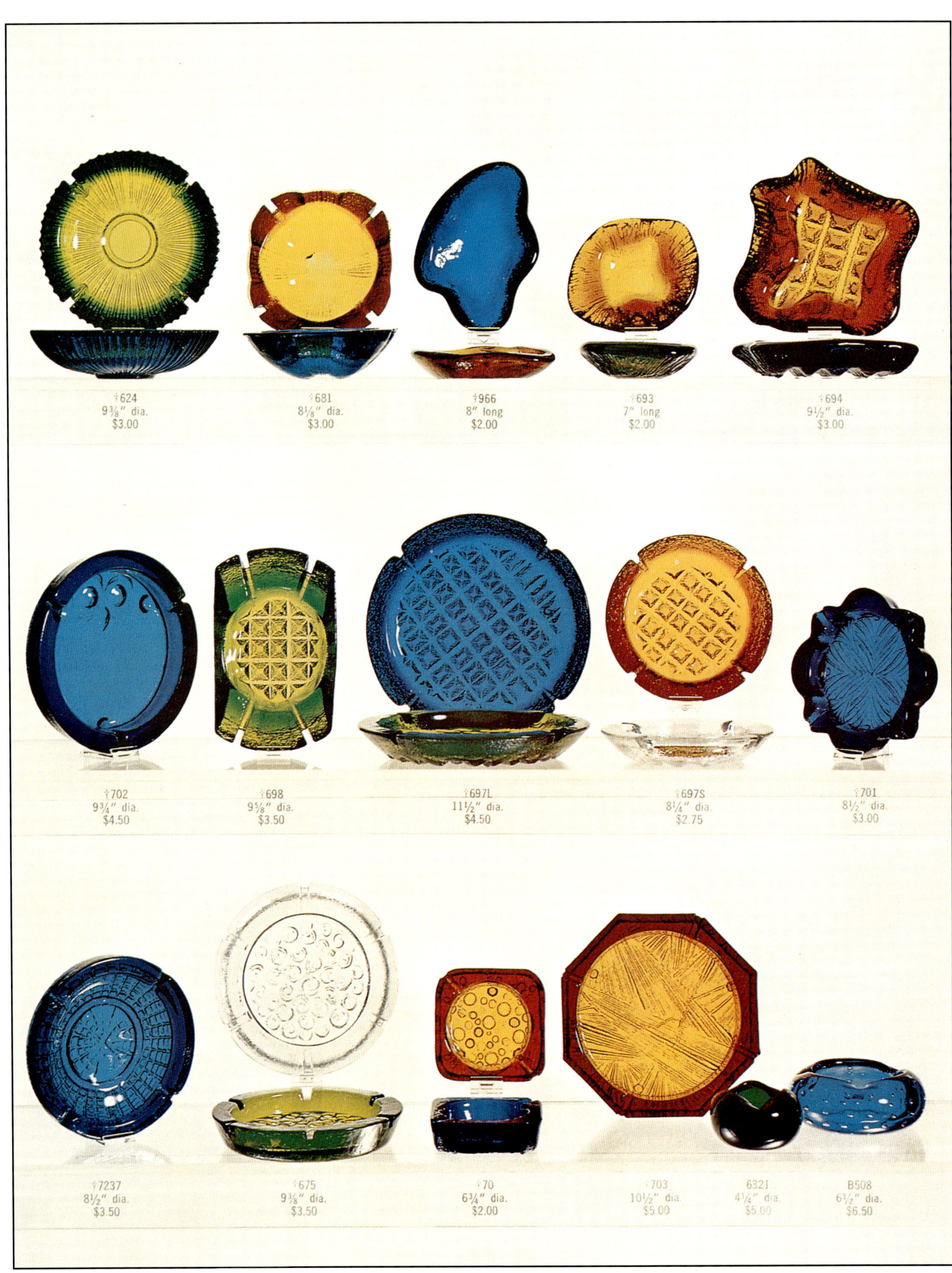

†624
9⅜″ dia.
$3.00

†681
8⅛″ dia.
$3.00

†966
8″ long
$2.00

†693
7″ long
$2.00

†694
9½″ dia.
$3.00

†702
9¾″ dia.
$4.50

†698
9⅝″ dia.
$3.50

†697L
11½″ dia.
$4.50

†697S
8¼″ dia.
$2.75

†701
8½″ dia.
$3.00

†7237
8½″ dia.
$3.50

†675
9⅜″ dia.
$3.50

†70
6¾″ dia.
$2.00

†703
10½″ dia.
$5.00

6321
4¼″ dia.
$5.00

B508
6½″ dia.
$6.50

without stopper
$17.50
7054
33" high
$30.00
7235
46" high
$35.00
6138W/S
35¾" high
$20.00
7236
27" tall
$17.50

7230
16½" high
$10.00
*7143S
6½" high
$5.00
*7143L
12½" high
$7.50
*7143M
8½" high
$6.00
7225
13½" high
$12.00
7125
14½" high
$12.00
7232
15" dia.
$12.00
*7116
6½" high
$7.50
*7128L
10" high
$10.00
*7128S
8" high
$8.00
7122
9½" high
$15.00
†633
14" long
$6.00
*7115S
5½" high
$5.00
*7115L
8" high
$7.00
*7115M
6½" high
$6.00
*7137
10½" dia.
$6.00

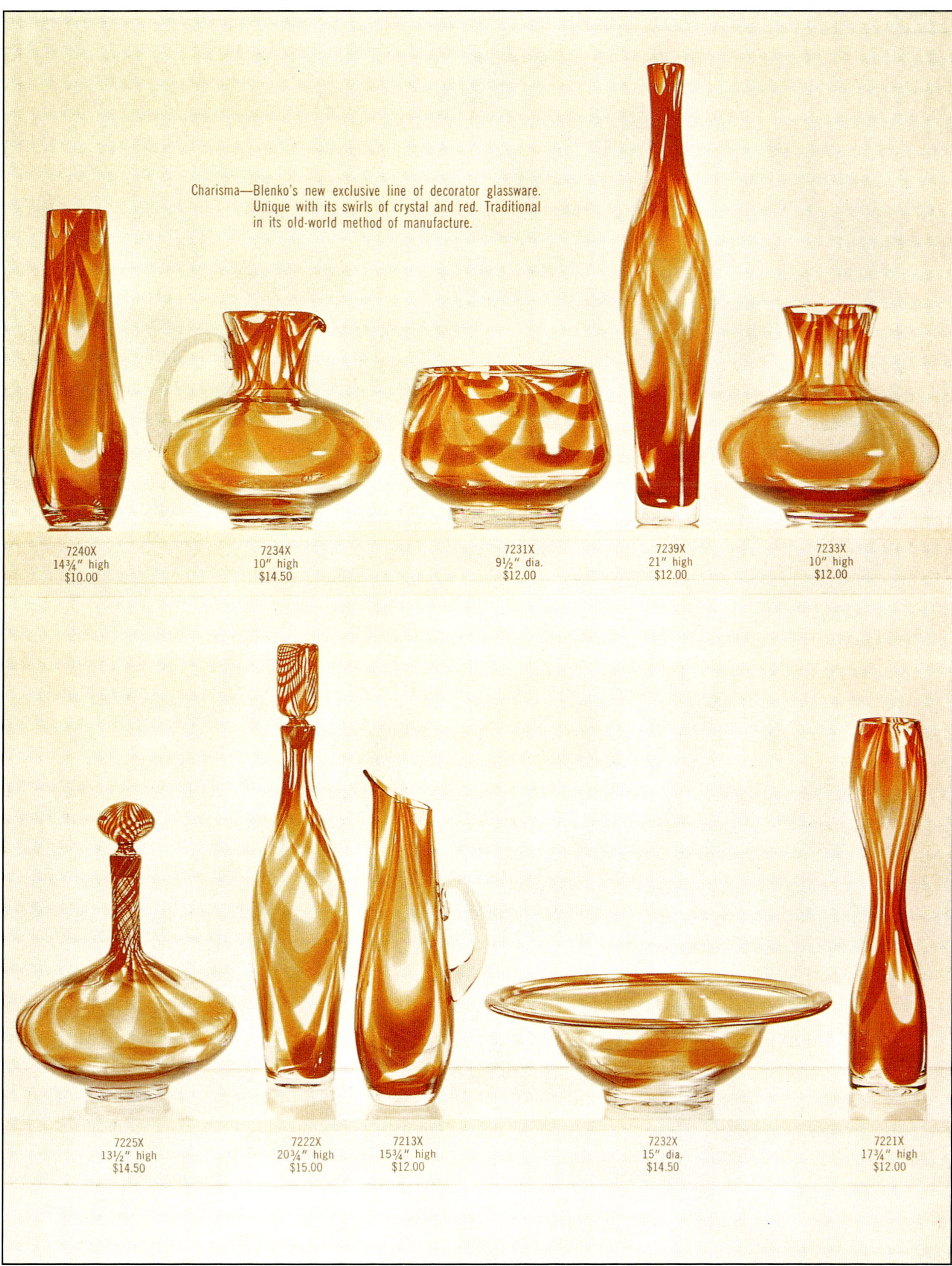

Charisma—Blenko's new exclusive line of decorator glassware. Unique with its swirls of crystal and red. Traditional in its old-world method of manufacture.

7240X 14¾″ high $10.00

7234X 10″ high $14.50

7231X 9½″ dia. $12.00

7239X 21″ high $12.00

7233X 10″ high $12.00

7225X 13½″ high $14.50

7222X 20¾″ high $15.00

7213X 15¾″ high $12.00

7232X 15″ dia. $14.50

7221X 17¾″ high $12.00

7020L
assorted colors
approx. 3½″ high
$5.00 each
7020M
assorted colors
approx. 3″ high
$4.00 each
7020S
assorted colors
approx. 2½″ high
$3.00 each
Blenko mushrooms are made entirely by hand; each one is unique. They are available in a multitude of color combinations.
Paperweight
Measurements
Approximate
711A
6″ high
$7.50
725E
3½″ dia.
$6.00
711B
6″ high
$7.50
725A
3½″ dia.
$5.00
725C
3½″ dia.
$6.00
711F
6″ high
$7.50
725D
3½″ dia.
$6.00
725B
3½″ dia.
$5.00
725B
3½″ dia.
$5.00
711C
6″ high
$7.50 ea.

†65CP 8¼" dia. $3.50

†65LE 8¼" dia. $3.50

†65PS 8¼" dia. $3.50

†65SG. 8¼" dia. $3.50

†65GM 8¼" dia. $3.50

†65SC 8¼" dia. $3.50

†65CN 8¼" dia. $3.50

†65AQ 8¼" dia. $3.50

†65TR 8¼" dia. $3.50

†65VR 8¼" dia. $3.50

†65AR 8¼" dia. $3.50

†65LB 8¼" dia. $3.50

68C 3¾" dia. $5.00

†68D 3¾" dia. $5.00

†68E 3¾" dia. $5.00

†68B 3¾" dia. $5.00

†68A 3¾" dia. $5.00

68F 3¾" dia. $5.00

68F 3¾" dia. $5.00

Paperweight measurements approximate

BLENKO
1973

TURQUOISE
CRYSTAL
WHEAT
EMERALD
OLIVE
TANGERINE
BLENKO COLORS 1973
† NUMBERS PRECEDED BY A DAGGER ARE NOT AVAILABLE IN TANGERINE.
*NUMBERS PRECEDED BY AN ASTERISK ARE AVAILABLE IN CRACKLED AS WELL AS PLAIN FINISH.
EACH PIECE IS AVAILABLE IN SIX COLORS, UNLESS MARKED OTHERWISE.

7328
12" high
$10.00
7213
15¾" high
$10.00
7222
20¾" high
$12.50
*7314
9½" high
$6.50
*736
7½" high
$5.00
7017
7¼" high
$4.50
7120
12½" high
$8.00
7323
13" high
$10.00
7127
13" high
$12.00
*729
11¾" high
$8.00
*727
8½" high
$7.00
7325
19" high
$12.00
†990A
3⅛" dia.
$1.00 ea.
*990
12" high
$8.00
Shade only
7048
19½" high
$18.50

*7313S
8½" high
$6.00

*7313L
10½" high
$7.50

*7224
15½" high
$10.00

6741
23¼" high
$16.00
Crystal stopper with tangerine and emerald bottles

*7228S
6½" high
$6.50

*7228LL
9½" high
$8.00

*7228M
7½" high
$7.00

*7228L
8½" high
$7.50

7316
8" high
$10.00

7114
16½" high
$12.50

*735
6½" high
$5.00

6212
20½" high
$12.00

7322
12½" high
$9.00

7326
19" high
$15.00

*629S
6" high
$7.50
*629
8½" high
$9.00
7329S
7" dia.
$4.00
7329L
12" dia.
$10.00
*738
8" high
$4.00
6716
14¼" high
$16.50
No tangerine or
emerald stoppers
7226M
16" high
$12.50
7226S
11½" high
$10.00
7051
21⅝" high
$14.00
*7227S
8" high
$6.50
*7227L
12½" high
$8.50
*7227M
10¼" high
$7.50

*971L
22" long
$31.50

*971M
16" long
$16.00

*5433
10" high
$14.00

*67S
15" high
6¾" dia. at base
$15.00
Crystal only

7231
9½" dia.
$10.50

*719
17" high
$8.50

*7312S
8½" high
$5.00

*7312L
10½" high
$6.50

7318
10½" high
$10.00

715
8" high
$6.00

6914
8" high
$5.00

6916
6½" high
$6.50

*7315
10" high
$7.50

*7324L
7" dia.
$8.50
*7324S
4½" dia.
$6.50
7033
16⅜" high
$10.00
6956
21" high
$14.00
7319
11" high
$8.50
6935
13½" high
$8.50
7327L
20" high
$15.00
7327S
18" high
$12.50
*726
7" high
$5.50
6942
11⅝" high
$8.50
6928
20¼" high
$10.50
7321
11" high
$10.00
6951
24" high
$14.00

No tangerine or
emerald stoppers
7029
16½" high
$10.00
6953
21" high
$15.00
*722M
8" high
$6.00
6810
10¾" high
$6.00
6952
13" high
$11.00
6955
22¾" high
$18.00
7223
25" high approx.
$10.00
7320
12" high
$10.00
706
6¾" high
$4.00
709
6¾" high
$5.50
7049
22" high
$15.00
6954
27¼" high
$16.00

6511
9½" high
$6.00
*3750L
5½" high
$5.50
*64B
1" high
$3.00
*739
7" high
$4.00
721
5½" high
$3.00
*7116
6½" high
$7.50
*6714
9¾" high
$8.50
*418S
4½" high
$2.25
*418L
6" high
$2.25
*6516
14½" high
$8.50
*636S
8" high
$6.00
*7018
13⅜" high
$7.00
*7126
14" high
$10.50
723
4½" high
$4.00
*6424
5" high
$3.00
*708
7 5/16" high
$4.00
*7141
9" high
$5.50
*6944
9½" high
$6.50
Lid Crystal only
*7210
8" high
$8.50
64D
11" high
$3.00
*705
6⅛" high
$3.00
Plate in color
7317
7" high
$10.00
7311
4¾" high
$5.00
7310
5" high
$5.00
*713
10½" high
$4.50
*7117
8" high
$6.50

51S
bubbles only
3" dia.
$9.00 doz.
51L
bubbles only
6" dia.
$24.00 doz.
51M
bubbles only
4½" dia.
$15.60 doz.
°6840
6" high
15½" dia.
$12.00
59
Mixed colors only
$1.00 box
°7028
5" high
11" dia.
$7.50
472
$1.50 box
°6950
7¾" high
$10.00
°37
13" high
$8.00
°49
10½" high
$8.00
384
7½" high
$3.50
°737
7" high
$4.00
°388
7½" high
$7.50
6320
3¼" dia.
$6.00
7017
7¼" high
$4.50
†7333
5" high
$6.50 pr.
†699B
6½" high
$6.50 pr.
†699A
6½" high
$6.50 pr.
†6813
7" high
$6.50 pr.
†6725
3½" high
3¾" wide
$6.50 pr.
†434
5½" high
$6.50 pr.

without stopper
$17.50
7054
33" high
$30.00
7235
46" high
$35.00
7334
29½" high
$25.00
7335
25½" high
$20.00
6138W/S
35¾" high
$20.00
7236
27" tall
$17.50

*7115M
6½" high
$6.00
*7115S
5½" high
$5.00
7331
18" dia.
$12.50
*7115L
8" high
$7.00
7225
13½" high
$12.00
*7137
10½" dia.
$6.00
*3744X
7" dia.
$4.00
7330L
9½" high
$9.00
+633
14" long
$6.00
7232
15" dia.
$12.00
7330S
6" high
$6.00
7330M
8" high
$7.50

BLENKO 1974

WHEAT
TANGERINE
CRYSTAL
PINE
TURQUOISE
OLIVE
BLENKO COLORS 1974
†NUMBERS PRECEDED BY A DAGGER ARE NOT AVAILABLE IN TANGERINE.
*NUMBERS PRECEDED BY AN ASTERISK ARE AVAILABLE IN CRACKLED AS WELL AS PLAIN FINISH.
EACH PIECE IS AVAILABLE IN SIX COLORS, UNLESS MARKED OTHERWISE.

*7411
13½" high
$8.00
7328
12" high
$12.00
7222
20¾" high
$12.50
*745
6" high
$7.00
*747
12" high
$6.50
*7017
7¼" high
$5.00
7323
13" high
$10.00
*7419
11" high
$6.50
*7418
10" high
$7.50
*727
8½" high
$7.00
*7314
9½" high
$6.50
*746
5½" high
$6.00
†990A
3⅛" dia.
$1.00 ea.
†990B
3⅛" dia.
$1.00 ea.
*990
12" high
$8.00
7048
19½" high
$18.50

*7313L 10½" high $7.50

7414 16½" high $12.00

*7313S 8½" high $6.00

6741 23¼" high $16.50 Crystal stopper with tangerine bottle

*749S 11½" high $6.00

*749L 17½" high $10.00

*749M 14½" high $8.00

7326 19" high $16.00

6212 20½" tall $12.50

7322 12½" high $9.50

*735 6½" high $5.00

7114 16½" high $12.50

7425S 10½" high $7.50

7425L 12½" high $9.00

*629S
6" high
$7.50
*629
8½" high
$10.00
*7426L
5¾" high
$10.00
*7426S
3¾" high
$4.50
*744
7" high
$7.00
6716
14¼" high
$17.50
Crystal stopper with
tangerine bottle
*7421
5" high
$6.50
7226M
16" high
$12.50
7226S
11½" high
$10.00
7051
21⅝" high
$15.00
*7417
10¾" high
$6.50
*7423
10¾" high
$12.50

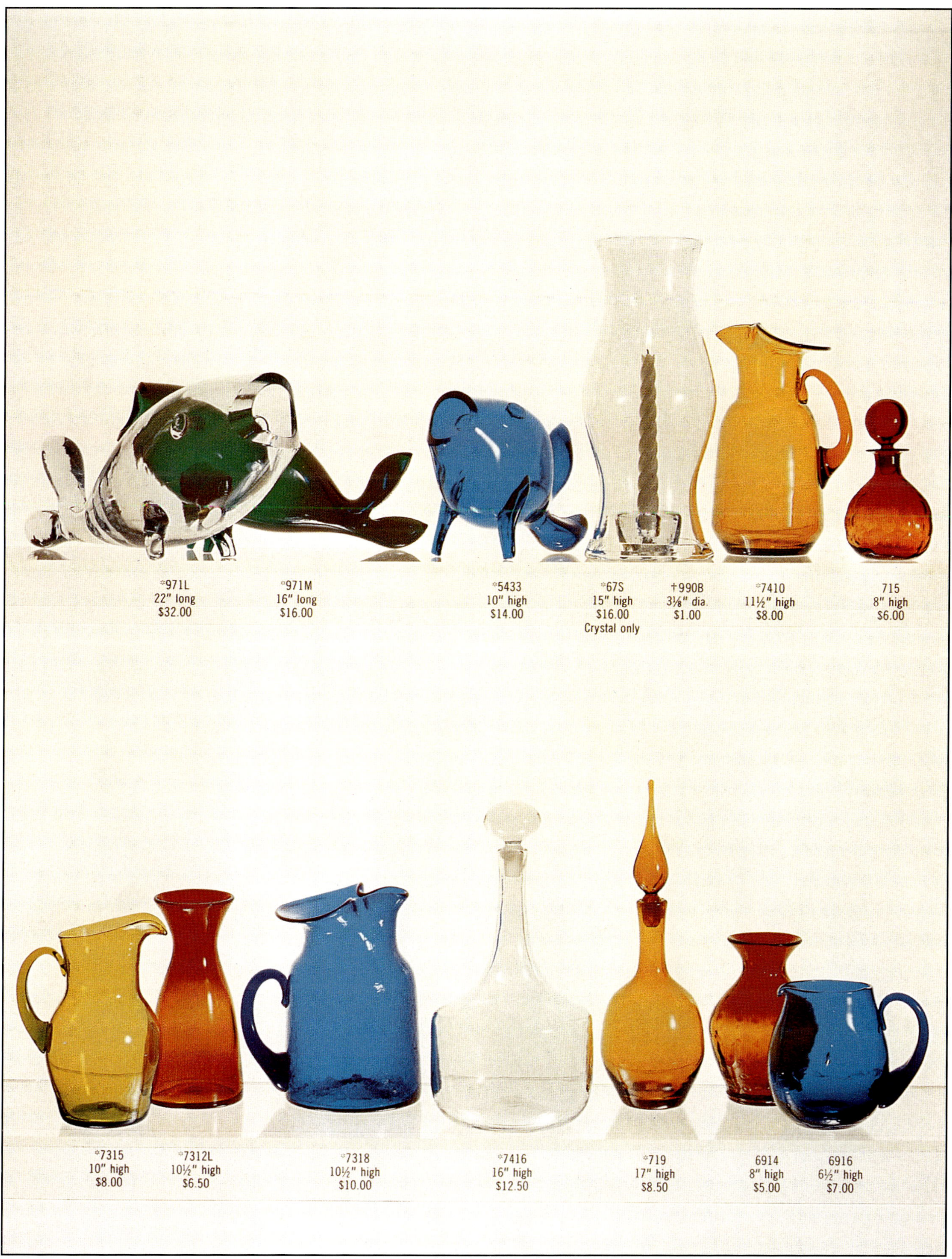

*971L 22" long $32.00

*971M 16" long $16.00

*5433 10" high $14.00

*67S 15" high $16.00 Crystal only

†990B 3⅛" dia. $1.00

*7410 11½" high $8.00

715 8" high $6.00

*7315 10" high $8.00

*7312L 10½" high $6.50

*7318 10½" high $10.00

*7416 16" high $12.50

*719 17" high $8.50

6914 8" high $5.00

6916 6½" high $7.00

7225
13½" high
$12.50
6935
13½" high
$9.00
6956
21" high
$15.00
7033
16⅜" high
$12.00
*726
7" high
$5.50
7321
11" high
$10.00
7327S
18" high
$14.00
7327L
20" high
$16.50
7319
11" high
$8.50
6928
20¼" high
$12.00
6942
11⅝" high
$9.00
6951
24" high
$15.00

7413
14½" high
$10.00
*7415
11¾" high
$10.00
709
6¾" high
$5.50
6953
21" high
$16.00
Crystal stopper with
tangerine bottle
6952
13" high
$12.00
6955
22¾" high
$20.00
7223
25" high
$10.00
7029
16½" high
$10.50
706
6¾" high
$4.00
7049
22" high
$16.00
6954
27¼" high
$16.50

6511
9½" high
$6.50
*3750L
5½" high
$5.50
*722M
8" high
$6.00 ea.
*7311
4¾" high
$5.00
*7310
4¾" high
$5.00
*64B
10" high
$3.00
*6714
9¾" high
$9.00
*418S
4½" high
$2.25 ea.
*418L
6" high
$2.25 ea.
*6516
14½" high
$8.50
723
4½" high
$4.00
7428L
17½" high
$12.50
7320
12" high
$10.00
7428S
15" high
$10.00
*7116
6½" high
$8.00
*705
6⅛" high
$3.00
64D
11" high
$3.00
*636S
8" high
$6.00
68F
3¾" dia.
$5.00
*6944
9½" high
$6.50
*708
7 5/16" high
$4.00
*6424
5" high
$3.00
*713
10½" high
$4.50
*7117
8" high
$6.50

*6840
6" high
15½" dia.
$12.50
59
Mixed colors only
$1.00 box
*7028
5" high
$8.00
472
$1.50 box
*6950
7¾" high
$10.50
*742
7" high
$3.50
*37
13" high
$8.00
384
7½" high
$3.50
*743
6¼" high
$5.00
*7412
11" high
$7.00
*7420
8½" high
$6.50
*388
7½" high
$8.00
†7333
5" high
$7.50 pr.
†741
6" high
$7.50 pr.
†699A
6½" high
$7.50 pr.
†6813
7" high
$7.50 pr.
*49
10½" high
$8.00
†6725
3½" high
3¾" wide
$7.50 pr.
†434
5½" high
$7.50 pr.

7229S
12" high
$11.00

7229L
14½" high
$14.00

†702
9¾" dia.
$5.00

711A
6" high
$7.50

†732
10½" dia.
$4.50

†701
8½" dia.
$3.00

†70
6¾" dia.
$2.50

7332
Crystal only
21½" tall
$18.00

†7237
8½" dia.
$3.50

†703
10½" dia.
$5.00

*7427
12¼" dia.
$10.00

*748L
7" high
$5.00 ea.
$10.00 pr.

*7330L
9½" high
$10.00

*7424
13¼" high
$12.50

7422
9" high
$10.00

*7330S
6" high
$6.50

6810
10¾" high
$6.00

*3744X
7" dia.
$4.50

711B
6" high
$7.50

711C
5" high
$7.50

*7137
10½" dia.
$6.50

*7330M
8" high
$8.00

51M
4½" dia.
$1.50 ea.

51S
3" dia.
$0.75 ea.

51M
4½" dia.
$1.50

51L
6" dia.
$2.00 ea.

7430
20" high
$16.00

51L
6" dia.
$2.00 ea.

51S
3" dia.
$0.75 ea.

51M
4½" dia.
$1.50 ea.

51S
3"
$0.75 ea.

6138
without stopper
$19.00
7236
27" tall
$18.50
7054
33" tall
$30.00
7235
46" tall
$35.00
7432
38" tall
$25.00
6138W/S
35¾" tall
$22.00
7431
28" tall
$20.00

†681
8⅛" dia.
$3.50
†697L
11½" dia.
$5.00
†68E
3¾" dia.
$5.00
†68D
4¾" high
$5.00
†675
9¾" dia.
$4.00
†697S
8¼" dia.
$3.00
†68H
4¾" high
$5.00
†966
8" dia.
$2.50
†74
6¾" dia.
$3.00
*748S
5" high
$3.75 ea.
†633
14" long
$6.00
†966
8" dia.
$2.50
51S
3" dia.
$0.75 ea.
51M
4½" dia.
$1.50 ea.
51L
6" dia.
$2.00 ea.
51S
3" dia.
$0.75 ea.
7429
16¾" high
$12.50
51S
3" dia.
$0.75 ea.
51L
6" dia.
$2.00 ea.
51M
4½" dia.
$1.50 ea.
51S
3" dia.
$0.75 ea.

BLENKO
75

TANGERINE
WHEAT
CRYSTAL
OLIVE
TURQUOISE
BLENKO 75 COLORS
†NUMBERS PRECEDED BY A DAGGER ARE NOT AVAILABLE IN TANGERINE.
*NUMBERS PRECEDED BY AN ASTERISK ARE AVAILABLE IN CRACKLED AS WELL AS PLAIN FINISH.
EACH PIECE IS AVAILABLE IN FIVE COLORS, UNLESS MARKED OTHERWISE.

6138
without stopper
$22.00
7236
27" tall
$20.00
7054
33" tall
$32.50
7235
46" tall
$37.50
7432
38" tall
$27.50
6138W/S
35¾" tall
$25.00
7431
28" tall
$20.00

6741
23¼" high
$18.50
Crystal stopper with
tangerine bottle

°7412
11" high
$8.00

6212
20½" high
$14.00

7320
12" high
$11.00
Crystal stopper with
tangerine bottle

6716
14¼" high
$20.00
Crystal stopper with
tangerine bottle

6951
24" high
$17.50

6956
21" high
$17.00

7332
21½" high
$20.00
Crystal only

6914
8" high
$5.50

7048
19½" high
$20.00

*37
13" high
$8.50
6954
27¼" high
$18.00
*49
10½" high
$8.50
*7411
13½" high
$9.00
7225
13½" high
$14.00
Crystal stopper only
7033
16⅜" high
$14.00
*7314
9½" high
$7.50
7029
16½" high
$12.00
*64B
10" high
$3.50
384
7½" high
$4.00

715
8" high
$6.50
719
17" high
$9.00
6955
22¾" high
$22.50
6516
14½" high
$9.00
7321
11" high
$11.00
Crystal stopper only
6935
13½" high
$10.00
7114
16½" high
$14.00
706
6¾" high
$4.50
7419
11" high
$7.50
749M
14½" high
$9.00
64D
11" high
$3.50
749S
11½" high
$7.00
7510
14" high
$11.00

6953
21" high
$17.50
Crystal stopper with
tangerine bottle
*636S
8" high
$6.50
*7415
11¾" high
$11.00
Crystal stopper only
*7416
16" high
$14.00
Crystal stoppers only
7323
13" high
$11.00
*6944
9½" high
$7.00
6952
13" high
$13.00
7051
21⅝" high
$17.00
704
6" high
$3.50
6928
20¼" high
$13.00
*7223
25" high
$11.00

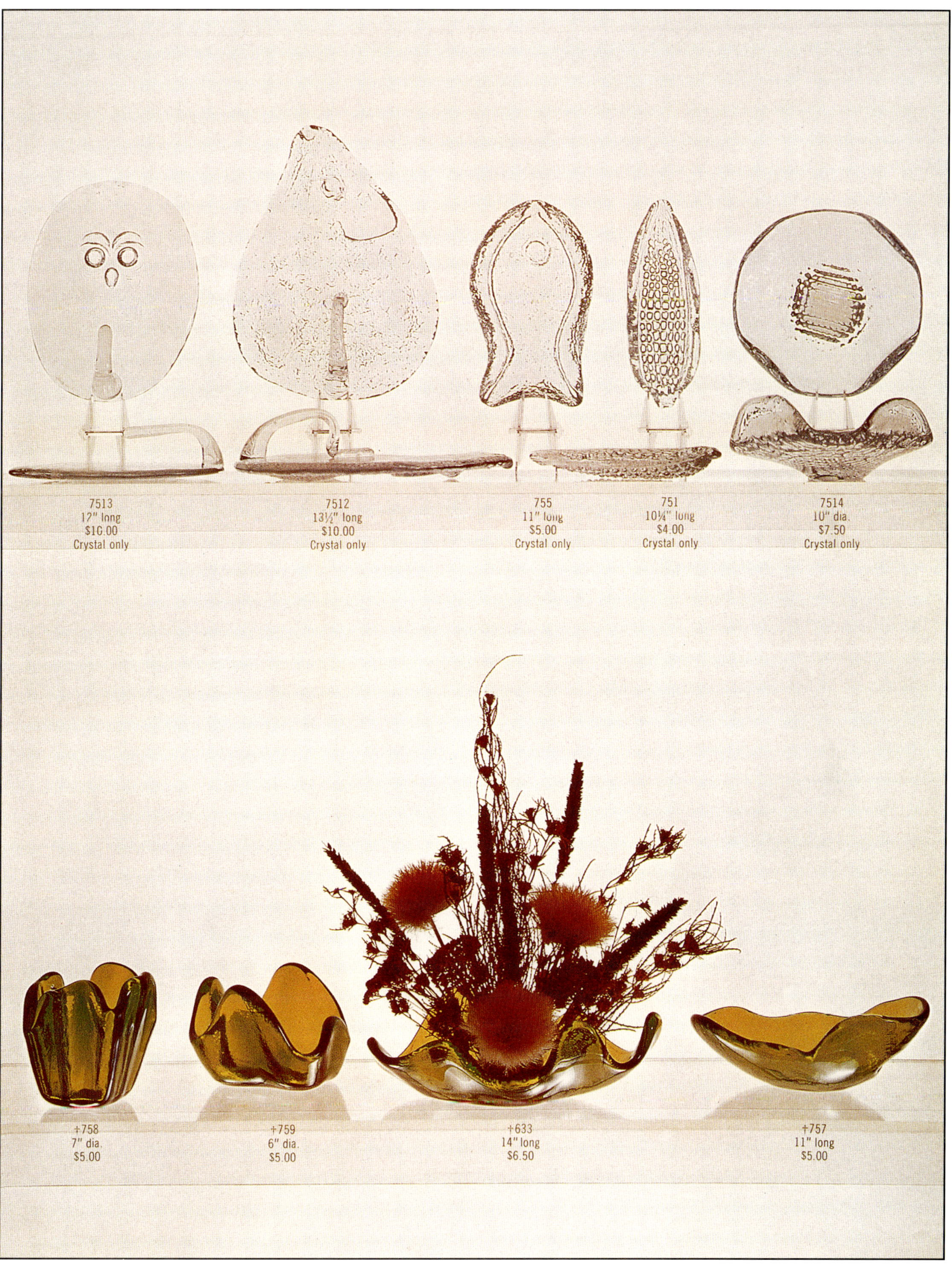
7513
12" long
$10.00
Crystal only
7512
13½" long
$10.00
Crystal only
755
11" long
$5.00
Crystal only
751
10¼" long
$4.00
Crystal only
7514
10" dia.
$7.50
Crystal only
†758
7" dia.
$5.00
†759
6" dia.
$5.00
†633
14" long
$6.50
†757
11" long
$5.00

7515L	7515S	7327S	7327L	7428	*6424	7425S
10" high	8" high	18" high	20" high	15" high	5" high	10½" high
$8.00	$6.00	$17.50	$20.00	$12.00	$3.50	$8.50

AMERICANA COLLECTION

*7226M	*7226S	*7410	*418S	*418L	*727	*7517L	*7522
16" high	11½" high	11½" high	4½" high	6" high	8½" high	7½" high	7½" high
$15.00	$12.50	$9.00	$2.50	$2.50	$8.00	$10.00	$4.00

7425L
12½" high
$10.00
7326
19" high
$20.00
7430
20" high
$22.00
6942
11⅝" high
$10.00
7519L
16" high
$12.50
7519S
12" high
$9.00
BLENKO 75
*7523
7½" high
$6.00
*7517S
5½" high
$7.00
*7524
5½" high
$8.00
*7520
7½" high
$7.50
7511
16" high
$15.00
7521L
14" high
$12.50
7521S
12" high
$10.00

7328
12" high
$15.00
7229L
14½" high
$15.00
7229S
12" high
$12.50
*7423
10¾" high
$13.50
*7116
6½" high
$8.50
*3750L
5½" high
$6.00
*7313L
10½" high
$8.00
*418L
6" high
$2.50
*418S
4½" high
$2.50
*7315
10" high
$9.00
*726
7" high
$6.00
*7028
5" high
$9.00
*6950
7¾" high
$12.00
*6840
6" high
15½" dia.
$13.50

*7424
13¼" high
$14.00
7518
12" high
$10.00
*629
8½" high
$11.00
*629S
6" high
$8.50
6916
6½" high
$7.50
709
6¾" high
$6.00
*7313S
8½" high
$6.50
6511
9½" high
$7.00
*6714
9¾" high
$10.00
*745
6" high
$7.50
*388
7½" high
$8.50
*7137
10½" dia.
$7.00
*3744X
7" dia.
$5.00
†6143S
5½" dia.
$1.50
†6143L
10½" dia.
$5.00

*5433
10" high
$16.00
*971M
16" long
$20.00
*971L
22" long
$35.00
+990B
3⅛" dia.
$1.50
*990
12" high
$8.50
*748L
7" high
$5.00 ea.
$10.00 pr.
+990A
3⅛" dia.
$1.50
7526
6½" dia.
$10.00
Made in
tangerine only
+7516
6½" dia.
$10.00
Not made in
tangerine
7527
6½" dia.
$10.00
Made in
tangerine only
7529
9½" high
$15.00
7528
7½" high
$15.00
7525
7½" high
$10.00
COLORS AS SHOWN ONLY
51M
4½" dia.
$1.75 ea.
51S
3" dia.
$1.00 ea.
51M
4½" dia.
$1.75 ea.
51M
4½" dia.
$1.75 ea.
51L
6" dia.
$2.25 ea.
51M
4½" dia.
$1.75 ea.
51L
6" dia.
$2.25 ea.
B508
6½" dia.
$7.50
6321
4¼" dia.
$5.00

711A
6" high
$8.00
711B
6" high
$8.00
711G
5" high
$8.00
711C
5" high
$8.00
+75C
3½" dia.
$2.50
+75A
3½" dia.
$2.50
+75B
3½" dia.
$2.50
68H
4¾" high
$6.00
+68A
3¾" dia.
$6.00
+68B
3¾" dia.
$6.00
+68D
4¾" high
$6.00
+68E
3¾" dia.
$6.00
68G
3¾" dia.
$6.00
68F
3¾" dia.
$6.00

BLENKO 76

6138W/S
35¾″ high
$36.00
without stopper
$30.00
7235
46″ high
$45.00
7432
38″ high
$38.00
7054
33″ high
$40.00
7628L
18″ high
$17.00
OLIVE
TURQUOISE
WHEAT
TANGERINE
CRYSTAL
BLENKO 76 COLORS
† NUMBERS PRECEDED BY A DAGGER ARE NOT AVAILABLE IN TANGERINE.
* NUMBERS PRECEDED BY AN ASTERISK ARE AVAILABLE IN CRACKLED AS WELL AS PLAIN FINISH.
EACH PIECE IS AVAILABLE IN FIVE COLORS, UNLESS MARKED OTHERWISE.

6741
23¼″ high
Crystal
stopper/w/
tangerine
bottle
$25.00
*7412
11″ high
$11.00
6212
20½″ high
$19.50
*7411
13½″ high
$11.50
715
8″ high
$8.00
6955
22¾″ high
$30.00
*6516
14½″ high
$11.50
6956
21″ high
$20.00
7510
14″ high
$17.00
*749M
14½″ high
$12.00
749S
11½″ high
$10.00
6914
8″ high
$8.00
704
6″ high
$5.00
7048
19½″ high
$28.00

6953
21″ high
Crystal stopper
with tangerine
bottle
$25.00
*636S
8″ high
$8.50
*37
13″ high
$11.00
7320
12″ high
Crystal
stopper
with
tangerine
bottle
$14.50
6716
14¼″ high
Crystal
stopper with
tangerine
bottle
$28.00
*719
17″ high
$11.50
*6944
9½″ high
$9.00
7114
16½″ high
$20.00
706
6¾″ high
$6.00
*7419
11″ high
$9.50
6952
13″ high
$18.50
6928
20¼″ high
$18.50
64D
11″ high
$5.00
*7223
25″ high
$14.50

6954
27¼″ high
$25.00
*49
10½″ high
$11.00
7225
13½″ high
Crystal
stoppers
only
$20.00
7621S
7½″ high
$8.00
7621L
11″ high
$11.00
7321
11″ high
Crystal
stoppers
only
$14.50
6951
24″ high
$25.00
6935
13½″ high
$14.00
7033
16⅜″ high
$20.00
7622L
18½″ high
$11.00
7622S
12½″ high
$8.00
7029
16½″ high
$16.50
384
7½″ high
$5.50
7051
21⅝″ high
$23.00
7623
16″ high
$11.00
*64B
10″ high
$5.00

7618
Approx.
6½″ high
Crystal
only
$14.00
7618
Approx.
6½″ high
Crystal
only
$14.00
7610
Approx.
7″ high
Crystal
Only
$14.00
7610
$14.00
7618
$14.00
7611
$9.00
7611
Approx.
5½″ high
Crystal
only
$9.00
†633
14″ long
$7.50
7610
$14.00
7619
Approx.
6½″ high
Crystal
only
$12.00
7511
16″ high
$23.00
*7639
8½″ dia.
$14.00
CRYSTAL PLANTATION
Smooth and textured crystal glass combines with leather hangers to give you a stunning grouping for your "Greenhouse" Department • The hanging planters are also self-standing and the hangers may be adjusted for level hanging.

7640M
15″ high
$20.00
as shown only
7640S
10″ high
$17.00
7640L
20″ high
$23.00
7641L
12″ high
$23.00
as shown only
7641S
9″ high
$17.50
as shown only
7643
7″ dia.
$11.00
7642
6″ high
$9.00
7645
11″ dia.
$17.50
7644
18″ dia.
as shown only
$23.00
the designer's group
Blenko is proud to present the handsome two-color contemporary "Designer's Collection".
Each piece is formed completely "off-hand" which means that no two pieces will ever
be identical • The Designer, Don Shepherd, will select the items for this collection, and
each piece will be dated and initialed to make it a unique creation with lasting value.

7614
11½" dia.
Crystal
only
$11.00
7616S
8" dia.
Crystal
only
$11.00
769
7" dia.
Crystal
only
$4.50
7612
4" high
Crystal
only
$7.50
† 767
7" dia.
$6.00
7615S
11½" dia.
Crystal
only
$10.00
7615L
14½" dia.
Crystal
only
$15.00
7613
12" dia.
Crystal
only
$10.00
7616S
8" dia.
Crystal
only
$11.00
7616L
11" dia.
Crystal
only
$15.00
†765
4½" dia.
$2.00 ea.
766S
7" dia.
Crystal
only
Sm. $4.00
766L
12½" dia.
Crystal
only
Lg. $15.00
768
13" long
Crystal only
$15.00
BLENKO'S
BOUNTY COLLECTION
Designs from nature's bounty of the land and seas are combined with beautifully wrought crystal glass to bring you the natural look in practical serving pieces.

7327S
18" high
$25.00
7327L
20" high
$28.00
7428
15" high
$20.00
7627
15½" high
$17.50
†7633
4½" high
$7.50
Americana
7628M
15" high
$15.00
*7638L
11½" high
$14.00
7629L
10" high
$14.00
7629S
8" high
$10.00
7631
8" high
$14.50
*7638S
9½" high
$10.00
7628S
10" high
$11.00
7630
8½" high
$11.00
BLENKO 76
Proudly Presents

*7624
7½″
Oil
$6.50
*7639
8½″ dia.
$14.00
*7632
12″ dia
$13.50
*7625
7½″ high
Vinegar
$6.50
*7524
5½″ high
$11.00
*7520
7½″ high
$10.00
7515S
8″ high
$8.00
*7637S
9″ high
$8.50
*7637L
11″ high
$11.00
Collection
7430
20″ high
$33.00
*6424
5″ high
$5.00
6942
11⅝″ high
$14.00
7634
3¾″ high
colors
$9.00
7635
7″ high
Crystal
only
$11.00
7636
5½″ high
Crystal
only
$11.00
7521S
12″ high
$14.00
7226S
11½″ high
$18.50
The character of the Founding Fathers of our country was reflected in the objects made and used in their time. Inspired by this bold, utilitarian tradition, Blenko's "Americana Collection" emerges as an important grouping for every store or shop emphasizing the Colonial look.
The authenticity which has been sought in this collection is reflected by the addition of tool marks, slight cords, and small bubbles that were characteristic of early handmade glass pieces.

7328
12" high
$23.00
7617
11" high
$14.50
7229S
12" high
$19.50
*7116
6½" high
$12.50
*3750L
5½" high
$8.00
*7313L
10½" high
$11.00
*418L
6" high
$3.00
*418S
4½" high
$3.00
*7315
10" high
$12.50
709
6¾" high
$7.50
*7028
5" high
$12.50
*388
7½" high
$11.00
*6950
7¾" high
$16.50
*6840
6" high
15½" dia.
$18.50

*7424
13¼" high
$20.00
7620
6½" high
$9.00
*629
8½" high
$15.00
*629S
6" high
$11.50
*7410
11½" high
$12.50
*418L
6" high
$3.00
*727
8½" high
$11.00
*418S
4½" high
$3.00
6511
9½" high
$10.00
*6714
9¾" high
$14.50
*745
6" high
$10.00
*7137
10½" dia.
$9.50
*3744X
7" dia.
$7.00
†764
9" long
$7.50
†6143S
5½" dia.
$1.75
†6143L
10½" dia.
$5.50

BLENKO
77

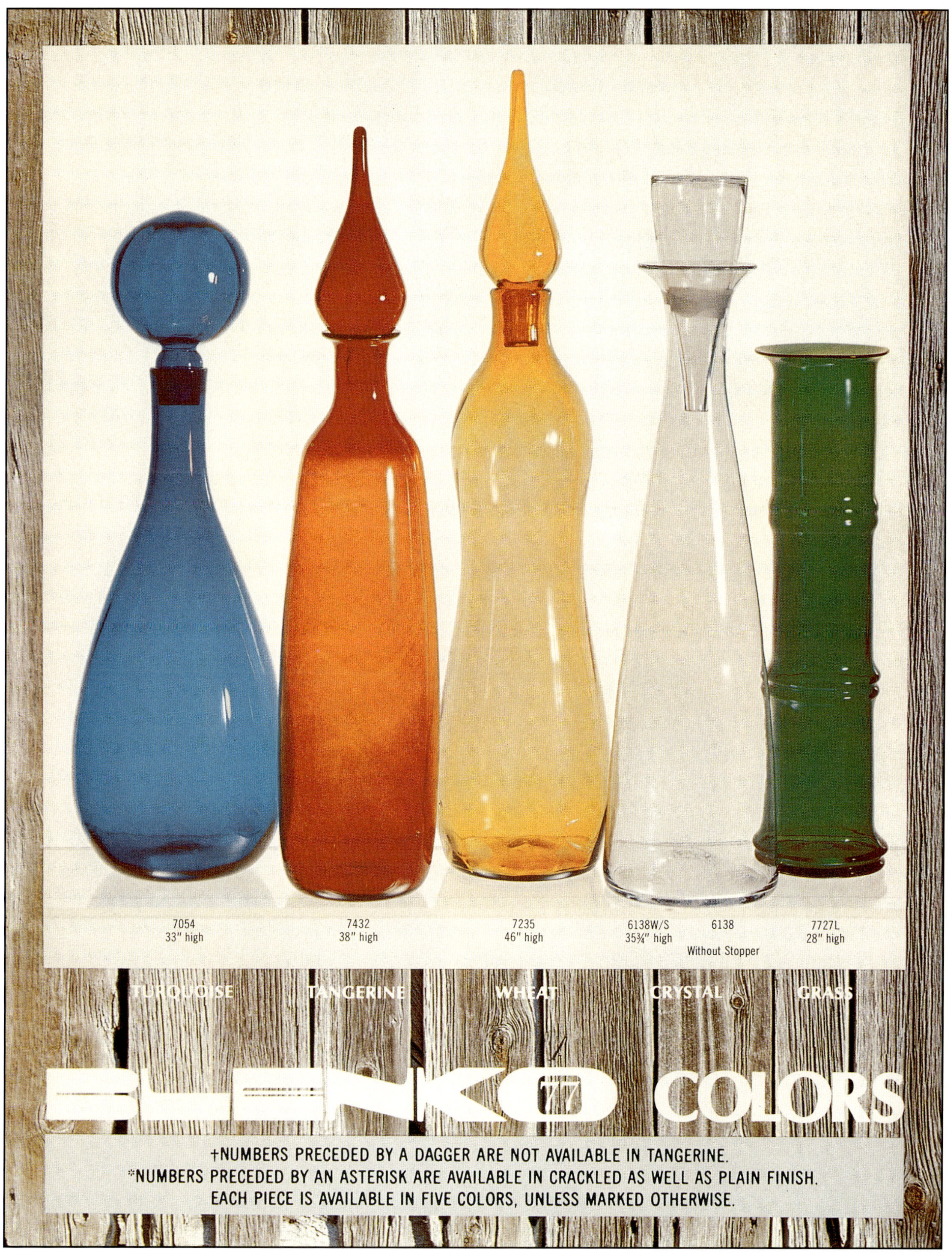
7054
33" high
7432
38" high
7235
46" high
6138W/S
35¾" high
6138
Without Stopper
7727L
28" high
TURQUOISE
TANGERINE
WHEAT
CRYSTAL
GRASS
BLENKO 77 COLORS
†NUMBERS PRECEDED BY A DAGGER ARE NOT AVAILABLE IN TANGERINE.
*NUMBERS PRECEDED BY AN ASTERISK ARE AVAILABLE IN CRACKLED AS WELL AS PLAIN FINISH.
EACH PIECE IS AVAILABLE IN FIVE COLORS, UNLESS MARKED OTHERWISE.

Crystal
stoppers
only
Crystal
stoppers
only
7618
6½" high approx.
Crystal only
7618
6½" high approx.
Crystal only
7225
13½" high
7720
9" high
7727S
15" high
+633
14" long
Oval
shape
7730
15¼" high
*64B
10" high
7051
21⅝" high
7623
16" high
*6944
9½" high
7048
19½" high
715
8" high
7728
15" high

6914
8" high
*7412
11" high
7726
15¼" high
704
6" high
384
7½" high
*636S
8" high
6212
20½" high
*49
10½" high
Crystal
stoppers
only
6954
27¼" high
7415
11¾" high
706
6¾" high
7725
16" high
6956
21" high
*749S
11½" high
*749M
14½" high

*7116
6½" high
*3750L
5½" high
7719
11" high
*7315
10" high
*727
8½" high
*418S
4½" high
6511
9½" high
Crystal
Stoppers
For
Tangerine
Bottles
Crystal
stoppers
only
7321
11" high
7511
16" high
64D
11" high
7620
6½" high
*7718
10" high
6741
23¼" high
6935
13½" high

*7410
11½" high
*418L
6" high
*418S
4½" high
*418L
6" high
*7313L
10½" high
7729
15¼" high
709
6¾" high
*6714
9¾" high
*745
6" high
7029
16½" high
778
4¾" high
*7419
11" high
7033
16⅜" high
*37
13" high
*719
17" high
*6516
14½" high

*388
7½" high
*6950
7¾" high
51S
3"
51L
6"
approx. dia.
51M
4"
59
Asst.
crystals
472
Solid or
mixed
†764
9" long
*3744X
7" dia.
*7137
10½" dia.
*6840
6" high — 15½" dia.
*7028
5" high
†6143S
5½" dia.
†6143L
10½" dia.
7512
13½" long
Crystal only
*629S
6" high
*629
8½" high

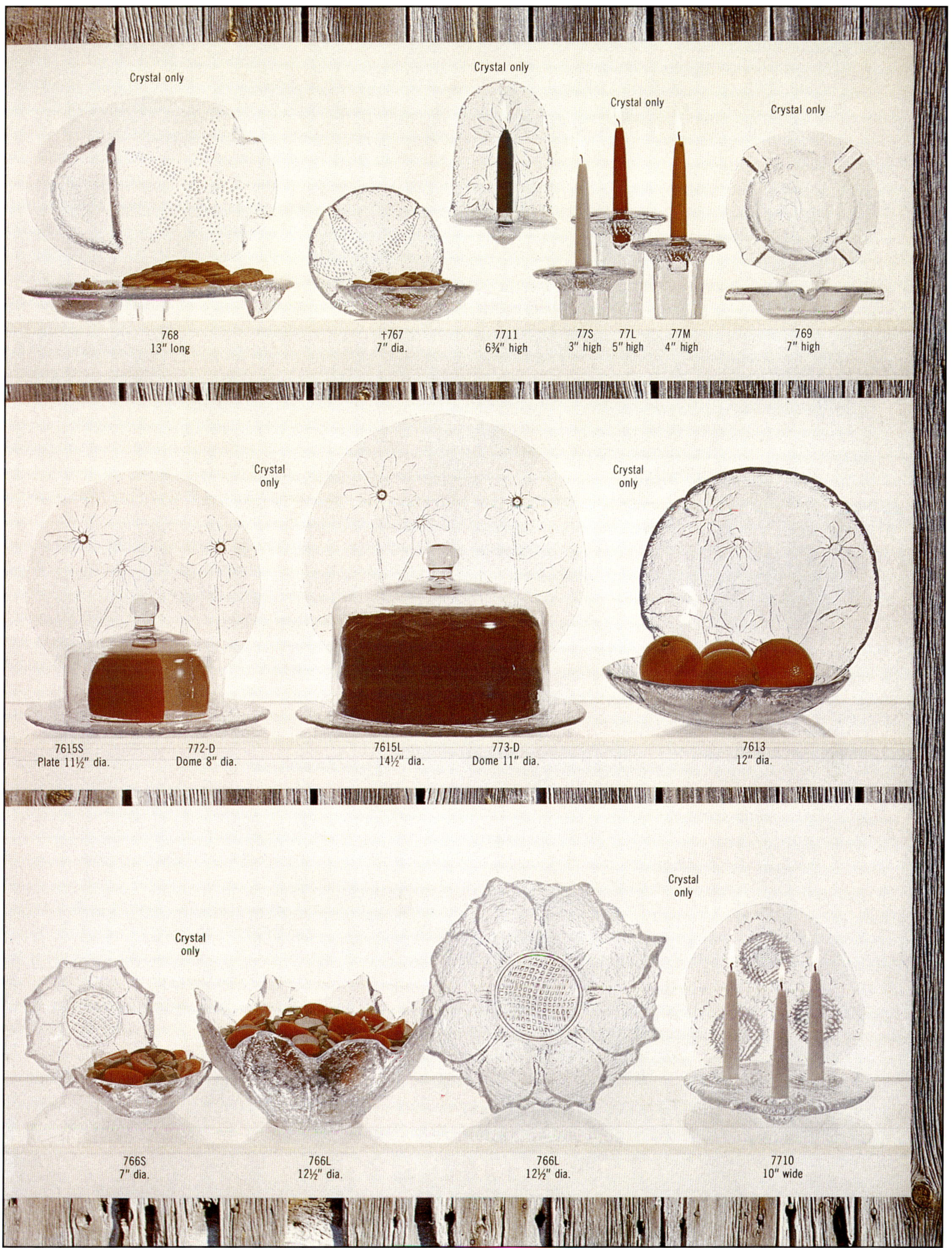
Crystal only
Crystal only
Crystal only
Crystal only
768
13" long
+767
7" dia.
7711
6¾" high
77S
3" high
77L
5" high
77M
4" high
769
7" high
Crystal only
Crystal only
7615S
Plate 11½" dia.
772-D
Dome 8" dia.
7615L
14½" dia.
773-D
Dome 11" dia.
7613
12" dia.
Crystal only
Crystal only
766S
7" dia.
766L
12½" dia.
766L
12½" dia.
7710
10" wide

"BLUE TOP MOUNTAIN GLASS"

Simple shapes that fit both country and contemporary decor. Available in crystal and wheat as well as blue top. Storage jar lids are natural finish Appalachian oak.

"CHIPS & DIPS &"

Smart crystal multi-purpose serving ware and storage jars complemented with single and double dip serving trays of natural finish Appalachian oak.

Americana Collection

"Chinese Classics"

BLENKO 78

6138—no stopper
789L—no stopper
7727L
28" high
WHEAT
6138W/S
35¾" high
TANGERINE
7235
46" high
GRASS
7054
33" high
CRYSTAL
789L-W/S
29" high
TURQUOISE
WHEAT
TANGERINE
GRASS
CRYSTAL
TURQUOISE
BLENKO 78 COLORS

*7639
8½" dia.
7029
16½" high
715
8" high
384
7½" high
*418S
4½"
high
*418L
6" high
*7313L
10½"
high
7727S
15"
high
7718
10"
high
7717
10"
high
No Tang.
Stoppers
*6714
9¾"
high
6741
23¼" high
*745
6" high
7048
19½"
high
7321
11"
high
*49
10½"
high
7720
9" high
7728
15"
high

crystal
stoppers
only
7225
13½"
high
6212
20½"
high
7721
8¼"
high
*7410
11½"
high
7327S
18"
high
*37
13"
high
*719
17"
high
*6516
14½"
high
51S 3" dia. approx.
*64B
10"
high
*749M
14½"
high
*636S
8"
high
*7419
11"
high
6956
21"
high
*6944
9½"
high
7511
16"
high
*6424
5"
high
7226S
11½"
high

*6840
15½" dia.
6" high
*3744X
7" dia.
*7137
10½" dia.
778
4¾"
high
709
6¾"
high
706
6¾"
high
6511
9½" high
51S – 3" dia.
51M – 4" dia.
51L – 6" dia.
(approx.)
*6950
7¾" high
7716
12" dia.
7723
13½" high
7632
12" dia.
7512
13½" long
Crystal only
766S
7" dia.
Crystal only
766L
12½" dia.
Crystal only
766L
12½" dia.
Crystal only

472
Solid
or
Mixed
59
Asst.
Crystals
*5433
10" high
*971L
22" long
(approx.)
*971M
16" long
(approx.)
7722
15" high
*7315
10" high
+6143L
10½" dia.
+6143S
5½" dia.
+633
14" long
(approx.)
*3750L
5½" high
*7116
6½" high
7615S Plate
11½" dia.
Crystal only
7615L Plate
14½" dia.
Crystal only
772D Dome
7½" dia.
Crystal only
773D Dome
11" dia.
Crystal only
7613 Shallow bowl
12" dia.
Crystal only

"BLUE TOP MOUNTAIN GLASS"

Simple shapes that fit both country and contemporary decor. Available in crystal and wheat only. Storage jar lids are natural finish Appalachian oak.

THE BLENKO GLASS COMPANY EMPORIUM

This year the Blenko Emporium features an exciting grouping called "HANDTIED GLASS". Designed as stringed pouches, this line includes vases, multi-purpose containers, pitchers, bowls, a decanter and ashtray with each piece being unique. Available in the full range of beautiful BLENKO colors.

BAMBOO
This popular theme has been developed into a handsome grouping available in the full range of BLENKO colors.
7821
6" high
7819
10½" high
1 Qt.
capacity
7821
6"
high
7818
6¼"
high
1 Qt.
capacity
7814
7" dia.
2¼" high
7817 Hurricane Shades
11" high
+990A Candleholders
3⅓" diameter
7816
3" dia.
candleholders
7820
10½" high
7815
6" high
7813
6½" high
7727S
15" high
7727L
28" high

CLASSIC

A contemporary designed grouping that is sure to become a "CLASSIC"—featuring a one-bottle wine decanter, one-bottle wine server, and a half-bottle wine server—with many other beautifully designed items available in the full range of Blenko colors.

7811
9½" dia.
5" high

788S
10" high
1 btl.
capacity

787L
8½" high
1 btl. wine
capacity

Wine
btl.
shown
not
BLENKO

787S
6½" high
½ btl. wine
capacity

7810
10" high
½ gal.
capacity

788L
11¾" high

787S
6½" high

Available with or without stoppers

789S
12¾" high
(with stopper
16¾" high)

789L
25" high
(with stopper
29" high)

789M
18¼" high
(with stopper
22¼" high)

786L
13" high

786S
11" high

CUMULUS

Crystal clear tops and cloud textured bottoms are the distinguishing features of this functional, contemporary grouping—available in crystal only.

"CHIPS & DIPS &"

Smart crystal multi-purpose serving ware and storage jars complemented with single and double dip serving trays of natural finish Appalachian oak.

BLENKO 79

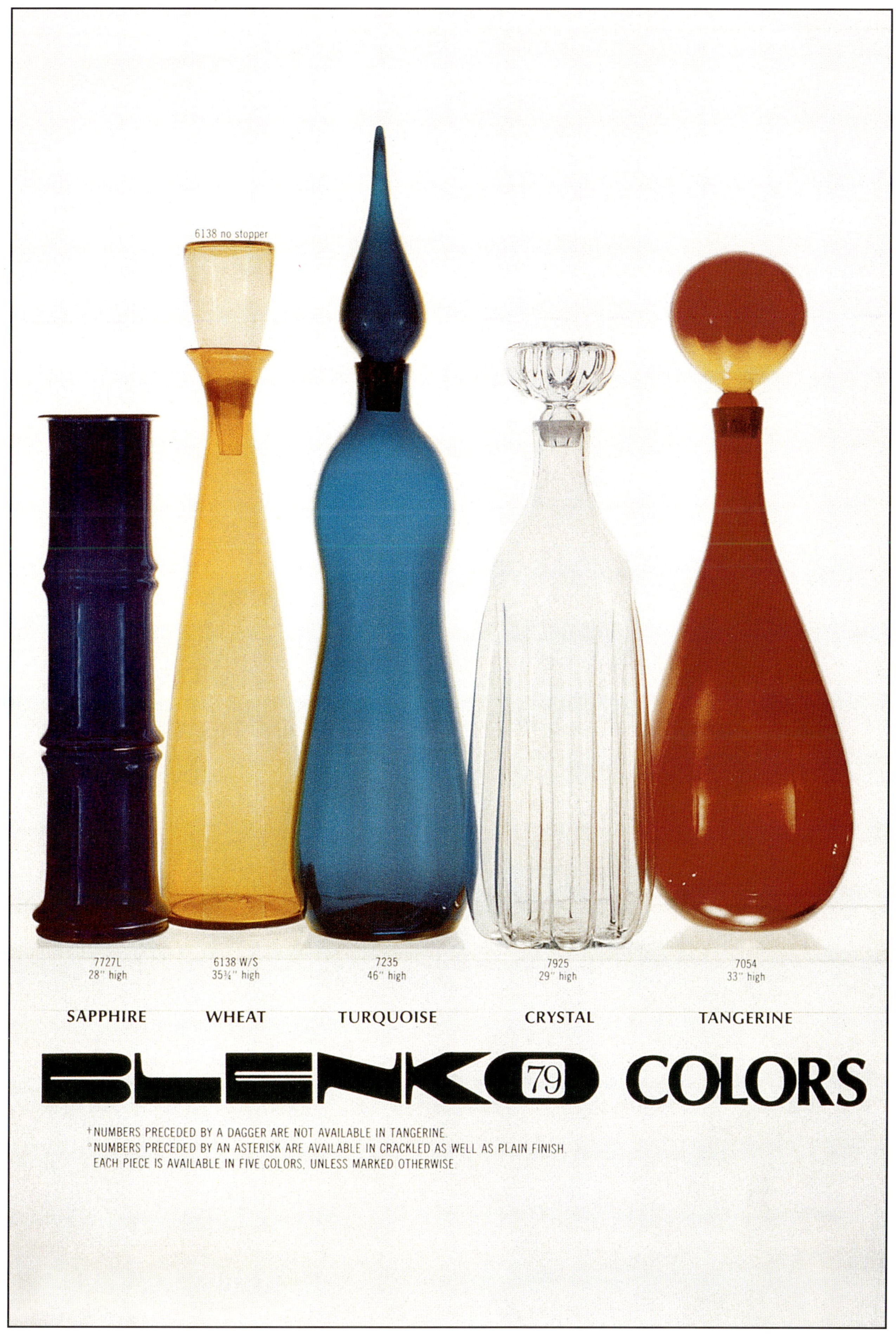
6138 no stopper
7727L
28" high
6138 W/S
35¾" high
7235
46" high
7925
29" high
7054
33" high
SAPPHIRE
WHEAT
TURQUOISE
CRYSTAL
TANGERINE
BLENKO 79 COLORS
†NUMBERS PRECEDED BY A DAGGER ARE NOT AVAILABLE IN TANGERINE.
*NUMBERS PRECEDED BY AN ASTERISK ARE AVAILABLE IN CRACKLED AS WELL AS PLAIN FINISH.
EACH PIECE IS AVAILABLE IN FIVE COLORS, UNLESS MARKED OTHERWISE.

RUFFLED GlaSS

An elegant grouping of flowing shapes including three sizes of bowls, a vase, and a basket. Available in all of the exciting BLENKO colors.

7918S
5½" high

7919
10" high
approx.

7918L
6" high
14½" dia.

7918M
7½" high

7920
8½" high

7918S
5½" high

7919
10" high
approx.

7918L
6" high
14½" dia.

7918M
7½" high

7920
8½" high

7918S
5½" high

7919
10" high
approx.

7918L
6" high
14½" dia.

7918M
7½" high

7920
8½" high

Barnwood

This simple textured glass line is designed as containers for liquids, flowers and fruits. Available in either crystal or wheat.

7911S
6" high

7911L
9½" high

7912L
10½" high

7912S
8" high
(Not Shown)

7910L
11" high

7910M
8½" high

7910S
6" high

7916
14" dia.

7914
8" high

7913
8" high

794
14" dia.

7915L
16" high

7915S
10" high

Handtied glass

Designed as stringed pouches, this line includes vases, multi-purpose containers, pitchers, bowls, a decanter and an ashtray with each piece being unique. Available in the full range of beautiful BLENKO colors.

7833
8½" high

785
7" dia.
2½" deep

7837
5" high

7839
6" high
8" dia.

7838
11½" dia.
5½" high

7835
8½" high
½ gal. capacity

*418S
4½" high

*418L
6" high

7836
12" high

7831
7½" high
1 qt. capacity

7837 (boxed)
5" high

7834
14½" high

7832
6½" high

7833
8½" high

7838
11½" dia.
5½" high

†*5433
10" high
(not made in tangerine)
51M
4" dia.
approx.
51S (in fish)
3" dia.
approx.
†*971L
22" approx.
(not made in tangerine)
51L 6" dia.
approx.
†*971M
16" approx.
(not made in tangerine)
*6950
7¾" high
51S
3" dia.
approx.
51M
4" dia.
approx.
*7928S
8¼" high
8" dia.
approx.
*7928L
12" high
11" dia.
approx.
*7928M
9¾" high
9½" dia.
approx.
7741L
10½" high
7741M
9½" high
7741S
8½" high
crystal
and
wheat
only
7732
12⅜" dia.
crystal
and
wheat
only
7738
16" high
7739L
11¼" high
crystal
and
wheat
only

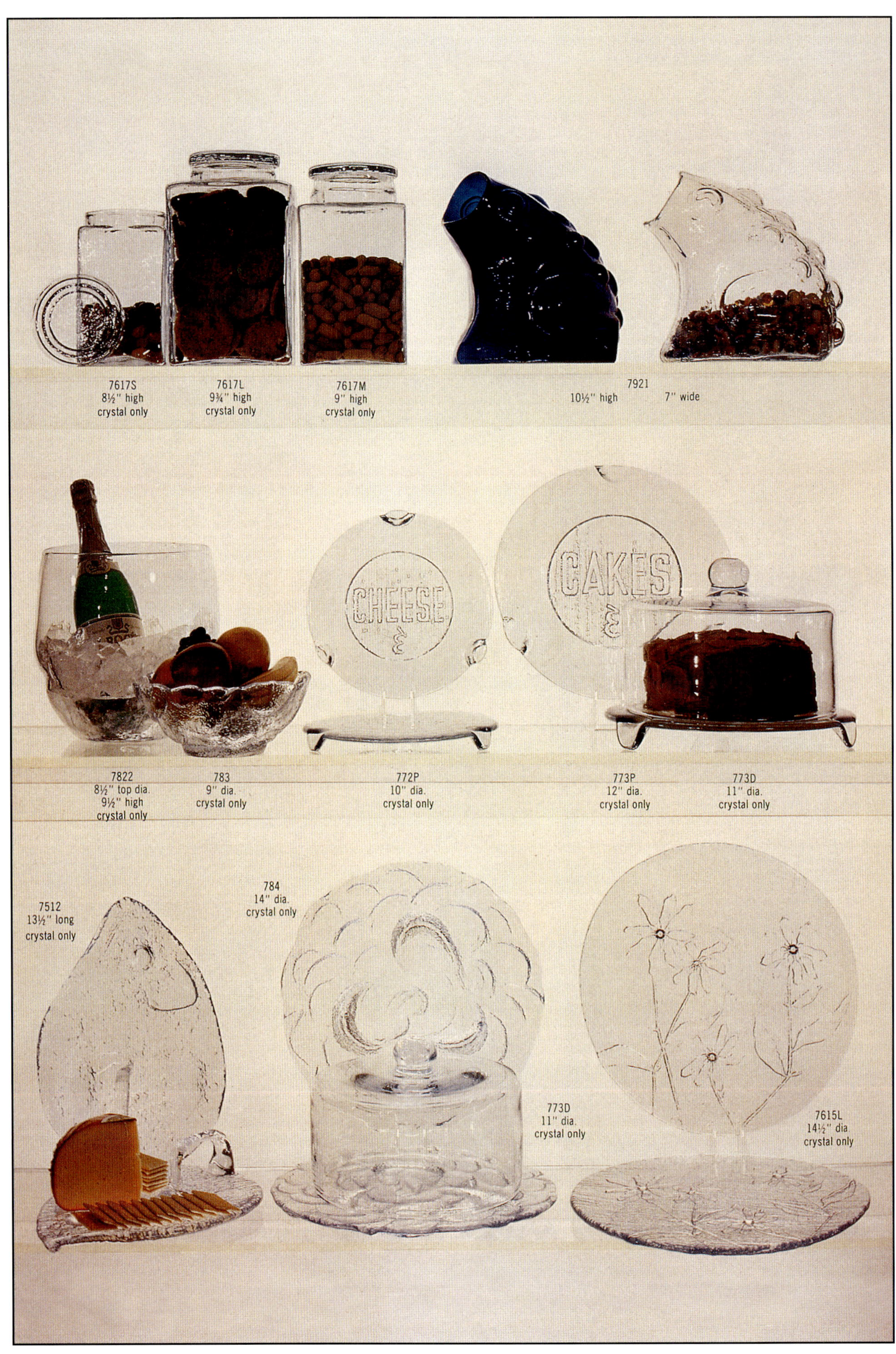

7617S
8½" high
crystal only
7617L
9¾" high
crystal only
7617M
9" high
crystal only
7921
10½" high
7" wide
CHEESE
CAKES
7822
8½" top dia.
9½" high
crystal only
783
9" dia.
crystal only
772P
10" dia.
crystal only
773P
12" dia.
crystal only
773D
11" dia.
crystal only
7512
13½" long
crystal only
784
14" dia.
crystal only
773D
11" dia.
crystal only
7615L
14½" dia.
crystal only

†966
Assorted Shapes
Approximately 8" dia.
Colors available only as shown
or solid crystal.
793 Ashtrays Individually Boxed.
†793S
Sapphire
†793S
Wheat
†793S
Turquoise
†756
7" dia.
9½" dia.
9½" dia.
9½" dia.
10¼" dia.
793 Ashtrays
individually boxed.
†793L
Turquoise
†793L
Wheat
†793L
Sapphire
†782
9¾" wide
11¾" long
†7712 10¾" dia.
†703 10½" dia.

*6944
9½" high
*64B
10" high
*6424
5" high
715
8" high
*49
10½" high
*7116
6½" high
*3750L
5½" high
7823
11" high
crystal only
*37
13" high
7922
7½" high approx.
crystal only
*749M
14½" high
7825
12" high
crystal only
6741
23¼" high
No Tangerine Stoppers
*719
17" high
6212
20½" high
7924
23" high
7029
16½" high

709
6¾" high
*6840
6" high
15½" dia.
778
4¾" high
706
6¾" high
*7313L
10½" high
*6714
9¾" high
*745
6" high
*418S
4½" high
*418L
6" high
*6516
14½" high
384
7½" high
7720
9" high
7048
19½" high
*7315
10" high
7327S
18" high
6956
21" high
7728
15" high

BLENKO
80

789L
25" high
SAPPHIRE
7727L
28" high
Boxed
ANTIQUE GREEN
7054
33" high
TANGERINE
6138
28" high
WHEAT
7924
23" high
Boxed
CRYSTAL
BLENKO 80 COLORS
†NUMBERS PRECEDED BY A DAGGER ARE NOT AVAILABLE IN TANGERINE.
*NUMBERS PRECEDED BY AN ASTERISK ARE AVAILABLE IN CRACKLED AS WELL AS PLAIN FINISH.
EACH PIECE IS AVAILABLE IN FIVE COLORS, UNLESS MARKED OTHERWISE.

RUFFLED Glass
An elegant grouping of flowing shapes including three sizes of bowls, a vase, and a basket. Available in all of the exciting BLENKO colors. Sizes approximate.
7918S 5½" high
7919 10" high
7918L 6" high 14½" dia.
7918M 7½" high
7920 8½" high
7918S 5½" high
7919 10" high
7918L 6" high 14½" dia.
7918M 7½" high
7920 8½" high
7918S 5½" high
7919 10" high
7918L 6" high 14½" dia.
7918M 7½" high
7920 8½" high

DIAMONDS
Multi-faceted in design and appearance, DIAMONDS is BLENKO's sparkling new line for 1980. Like the gem, DIAMONDS show excellent investment potential. Available in crystal only.
806S
8" high
8010
7¼" x 13" D.
803
5" dia.
1½" high
809
10" high
801
4½" high
808
11" hurricane
5" x 5" base
804S
5" x 5" x 1½"
804L
7" x 7" x 1½"
805
2" x 2" x 2"
802S
2½" x 2½" x 2½"
806L
13½" high
806M
9½" high
802L
2½" x
7½"
802M
2½" x 5"
802S
2½"
x 2½"
x 2½"
806S
8" high

Barnwood
This simple textured glass line is designed as containers for liquids, flowers and fruits. Available in either crystal or wheat.
7914
8" high
7914
8" high
*418L
6" high
*418S
4½" high
7911L
9½" high
7911S
6" high
7910M
8½" high
7910L
11" high
7910S
6" high
7913
8" high
7913
8" high
PENGUINS
Icy cool, in crystal or sapphire, cased in crystal with heavy sham heads, these elegant, animated creatures are available in two sizes.
8020L
14" high approximately
8020S
9½" high approximately

CHEESE
CAKES
772P
10" dia.
crystal
only
773P plate
12" dia.
crystal only
773D dome
11" dia.
crystal only
80L
4½" high
crystal only
80S
2¾" high
crystal only
766S
7" dia.
crystal
only
766L
12½" dia.
crystal
only
784
14" dia.
crystal only
†6143L
10½" dia.
†6143S
5½" dia.
7512
13½" long
crystal
only
783
9" dia
crystal only
7615L
14½" dia. crystal only
7615S
11½" dia.
crystal only

*8016S 8½" high
*8016L 12" high
*8016M 10½" high
*7928S 7¾" high
*7928L 10¼" high
*7928M 8¾" high

8021 14½" high
789S 12¾" high
789M 18¼" high
806S 8" high
7728 15" high

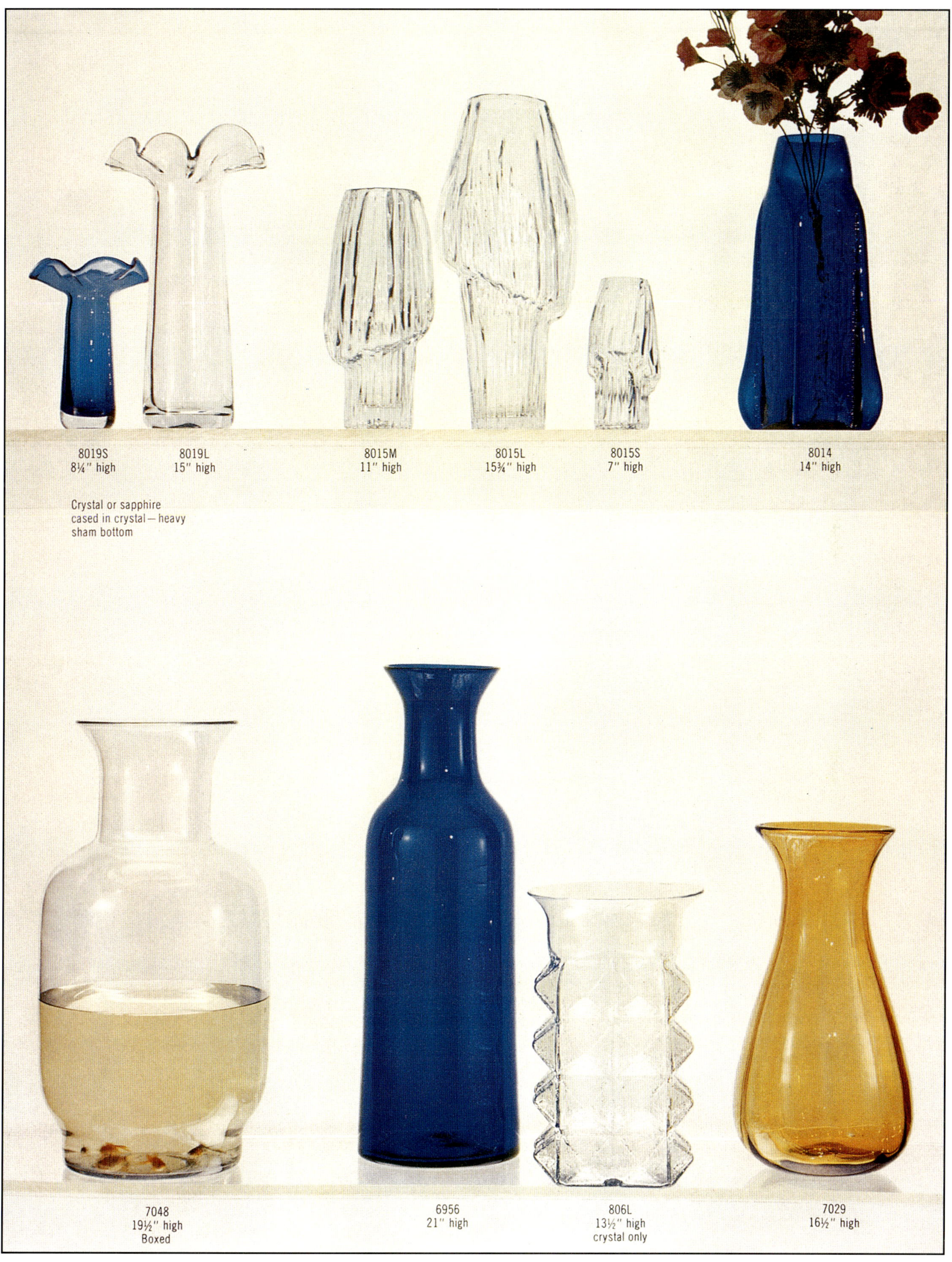
8019S
8¼" high

8019L
15" high

Crystal or sapphire cased in crystal—heavy sham bottom

8015M
11" high

8015L
15¾" high

8015S
7" high

8014
14" high

7048
19½" high
Boxed

6956
21" high

806L
13½" high
crystal only

7029
16½" high

8027
6" high
8026
11" high
472
solid
colors
or
mixed
in box
*8011
7" high
*8013
6" high
11¼" dia.
*8012
6" high
9" dia.
715
8" high
709
6¾" high
59
mixed
colors
only
472
solid
colors
or
mixed
in box
7922
7½" high approx.
crystal
or antique
green only
*37
13" high
*6424
5" high
*7315
10" high
*7927
8¾" high
*7926S
9" high
*7926L
11" high
*7926M
10" high
*749M
14½" high

8018
5" high
8017
9½" high
*6516
14½" high
807
6" high
*49
10½" high
*6944
9½" high
*745
6" high
*418S
4½" high
*418L
6" high
*7116
6½" high
*3750L
5½" high
706
6¾" high
*64B
10" high
778
4¾" high
7820
10½" high
7813
6½" high
7727S
15" high
7821
6" high
7818
6¼" high
7617L
10⅛" high
crystal only
7617S
8⅛" high
crystal only

†*971M
16" long approx.
†*971L
22" long approx.
This size boxed
†*5433
10" high approx.
†699A
6½" high
Boxed
†781
6" high
Boxed
†775
4¾" high
Not
Boxed
†6813
7" high
Boxed
†7333
5" high
Boxed
†434
5½" high
Boxed
384
7½" high
7738
16" high
crystal, wheat or
green only
7732
12⅜" dia.
crystal or wheat only
*418S
4½" high
*418L
6" high
*7313L
10½" high

designer's studio series:

is a group of vases in three shapes created by BLENKO's designer, Don Shepherd. Every piece is made offhand and is unique. The monogram signature of Don Shepherd along with the year (80) and the company name (BLENKO) are signed on the bottom of every vase and a personalized name tag will be shipped with each piece of glass.

Don Shepherd has been design director for the Blenko Glass Company since the fall of 1975. Not only is he recognized as a glass designer and artist, but he is also well-known for his work in architectural arts and environmental design. He is an exhibitor in the current exhibition, "New Glass—a World-wide Survey".

BLENKO 81

789L
25" high
ANTIQUE GREEN
7054
33" high
TANGERINE
8134L
33½" high
SAPPHIRE
7727L
28" high
(Boxed)
WHEAT
7924
23" high
(Boxed)
CRYSTAL
BLENKO 81 COLORS
†Numbers preceded by a dagger are not available in tangerine.
*Numbers preceded by an asterisk are available in crackled as well as plain finish.
Each piece is available in five colors, unless marked otherwise . . .

country ware
Rustic "Country Ware"
available in seedy crystal and seedy wheat only . . . . .
8140
3½" high
crystal
&
wheat
8128
5½" high
crystal
&
wheat
8125S
8½" high
crystal
&
wheat
8125L
10" high
crystal
&
wheat
8124S
8" high
crystal
&
wheat
8126
8" high
crystal
&
wheat
819P
13" dia.
crystal & wheat
8127
6¾" high
crystal
&
wheat
8124M
10" high
crystal
&
wheat
8124L
13½" high
crystal
&
wheat
811
3¾" high
crystal
&
wheat
7634
3¾"
high
8129
9½" high
crystal
&
wheat

FACET
Full color BLENKO line with crystal stopper only in the decanters . . .
8131L
13½" high
8131S
7½" high
8130L
9¼" high
1½ qt.
approx.
*418S
4½"
high
*418L
6" high
8130S
7¼" high
1 qt. approx.
†813
8¼" dia.
not made in
tangerine
8018
5" high
8133
8½" high
8132M
11½" high
8132L
19" high
8017
9½" high

*7928S
7¾" high
*7928L
10¼" high
*7928M
8¾" high
8134S
22½" high
8134L
33½" high
8134M
27½" high
8136S
15½" high
8136L
22½" high
8136M
18½" high

8121S 6" high

8121L 11" high

8121M 9" high

*8016M 10½" high

*8016L 12" high

*8016S 8½" high

8135S 16" high

8135L 23" high

8135M 19¼" high

8137S 17" high

8137L 24" high

8137M 20" high

706
6¾"
high
*6516
14½" high
crystal
stoppers
709
6¾" high
*8013
6" high
11¼" dia.
8120S
6" high
8120L
11" high
8120M
9" high
*49
10½" high
*37
13" high
472
solid colors
or
mixed in box
*6424
5" high
approx.
7914
8" high
crystal
&
wheat only
8122S
11½" high
8122L
14¾"
high
8122M
13" high
8132M
11¾"
high
crystal stoppers
7029
16½" high
8015L
15¾"
high
8015M
11" high

7918S
5½" high
7918M
7½" high
7919
10" high
7920
8½" high
*64B
10" high
7922
7½" high approx.
crystal or
antique green
only
7910L
11" high
crystal
&
wheat
7910M
8½" high
crystal
&
wheat
7732
12⅜" dia.
crystal or wheat
807
6" high
7728
15" high
*749M
14½" high
8021
14½" high
384
7½" high
8136S
15½" high

*818L
9⅛" high
½ gal.
approx.
*818S
6½" high
1 qt.
approx.
*418L
6" high
7911L
10" high
crystal
&
wheat only
½ gal. approx.
7911S
6" high
crystal &
wheat only
1 qt. approx.
*745
6" high
7818
6¼" high
*7315
10" high
*418S
4½" high
*7116
6½" high
*3750L
5½" high
7727S
15" high
789S
12¾" high
8138
14" high
7738
16" high
crystal wheat & ant. grn.

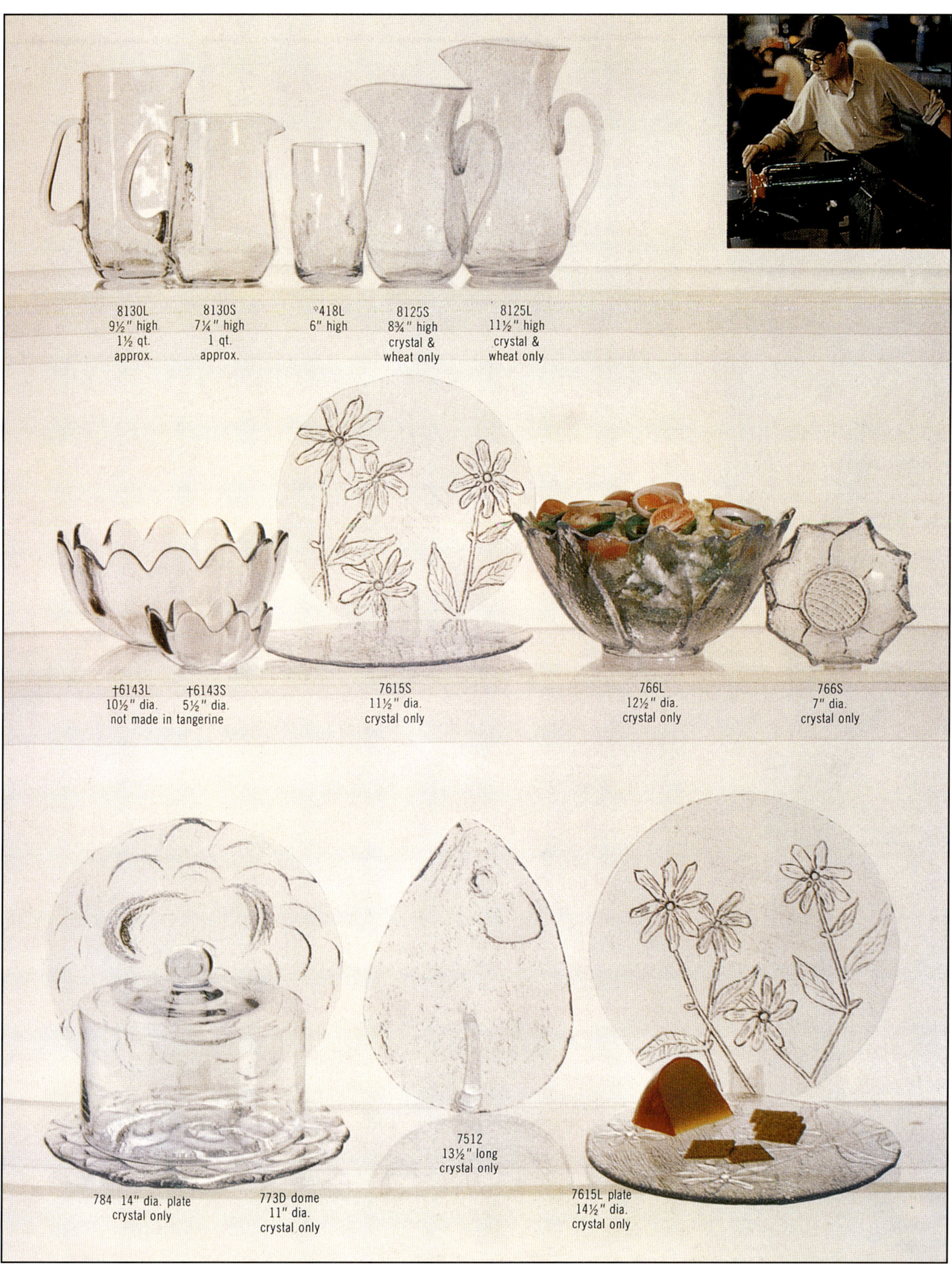

8130L
9½" high
1½ qt.
approx.
8130S
7¼" high
1 qt.
approx.
*418L
6" high
8125S
8¾" high
crystal &
wheat only
8125L
11½" high
crystal &
wheat only
†6143L
10½" dia.
†6143S
5½" dia.
not made in tangerine
7615S
11½" dia.
crystal only
766L
12½" dia.
crystal only
766S
7" dia.
crystal only
784 14" dia. plate
crystal only
773D dome
11" dia.
crystal only
7512
13½" long
crystal only
7615L plate
14½" dia.
crystal only

7634
3¾" high

811
3¾" high

802S
2½" x 2½" x 2½"
crystal only

802L
2½" x 7½"
crystal only

802M
2½" x 5"
crystal only

808
11" hurricane
5" x 5" base

789M 18¼" high

8139
23" high

6956
21" high

7048 19½" high
Boxed

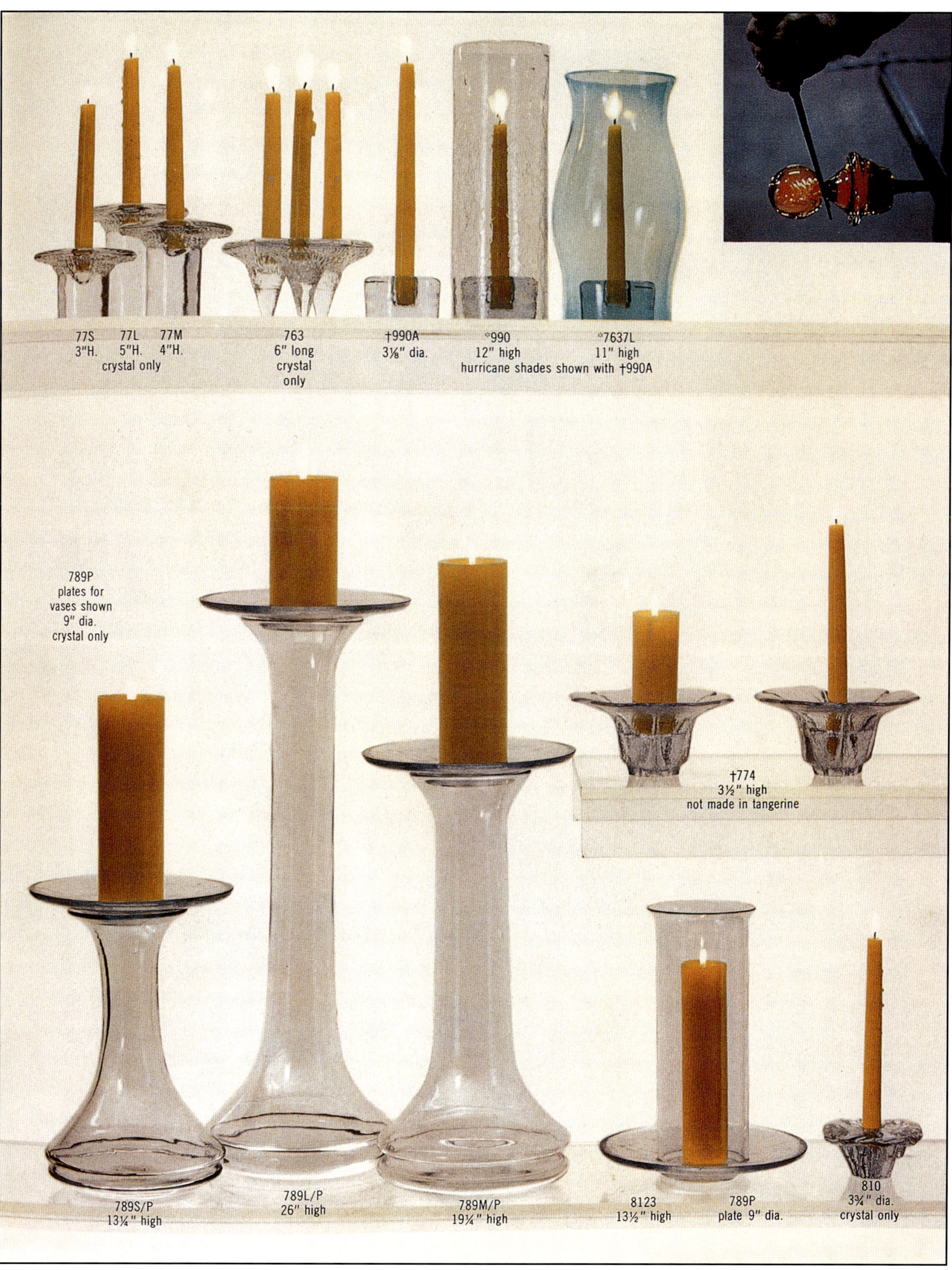
77S
3"H.
77L
5"H.
77M
4"H.
crystal only
763
6" long
crystal
only
†990A
3⅛" dia.
*990
12" high
*7637L
11" high
hurricane shades shown with †990A
789P
plates for
vases shown
9" dia.
crystal only
†774
3½" high
not made in tangerine
789S/P
13¼" high
789L/P
26" high
789M/P
19¾" high
8123
13½" high
789P
plate 9" dia.
810
3¾" dia.
crystal only

BLENKO 82

8137L
24" high
789L
25" high
7727L
28" high
boxed
7924
23" high
boxed
WHEAT
SAPPHIRE
ANTIQUE GREEN
CRYSTAL
BLENKO 82 COLORS
*Numbers preceded by an asterisk are available in crackled as well as plain finish.
All dimensions shown in catalog are approximate.

rock collection
Inspired by white granite rocks, these free-spirited, random shapes combine to form a stunning nature-scape of functional items—as shown only.
8213
paperweight
3 x 4
8217M
8 x 5½"
8213
paperweight
3 x 4
8214
candleholder
3¼" x 2"
8219L
bowl
10½" dia.
5" high
8219S
8 x 6
8215
3 x 4
vase
8216M
7½" x 7½"
8216L
9¼ x 9¼
8216S
5" x 4½"
8217L
11" x 6½"
8213
paperweight
3 x 4
8217S
5½" x 4¾"

Big Sky
Blue skies and green earth join with uniquely sculptured mountains to bring you this beautiful West Virginia "landscape" series of functional items. Also available in crystal.
8224
7½" high
8222
8" high
8223
4¾" high
8226
10¾" high
8227
9¼" high
Ice Bucket
8225
12½" high
8221L
12" high
8221S
9" high
8228
4½" high
14" dia.

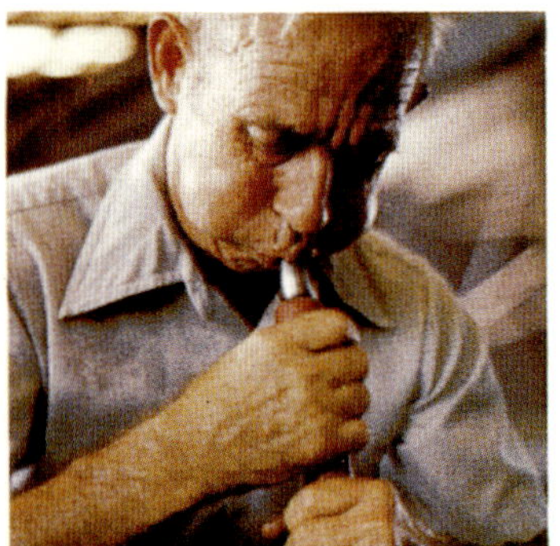

FACET

Full color BLENKO line with crystal stopper only in the decanters . . . All sizes approximate

813
8¼" dia.

8130S
7¼" high
Approx.
1 qt.

*418L
6" high

*418S
4½" high

8130L
9¼" high
Approx.
1½ qt.

8131S
7½" high

8131L
13½" high

8017
9½" high

8132L
19" high

crystal stoppers only

8132M
11½" high

8133
8½" high

8018
5" high

balloons
Blown up in glass, these festive pieces are the perfect containers for dried grasses and flowers.
828S 6¾" high Approx.
828L 11" high Approx.
828M 9¼" high Approx.
828S 6¾" high Approx.
828L 11" high Approx.
828M 9¼" high Approx.
The balloons are available in antique green/w/tangerine stripes only . . .
*7928M 8¾" high Approx.
*7928L 10¼" high Approx.
*7928S 7¾" high Approx.
8121M 9" high Approx.
8121L 11" high Approx.
8121S 6" high Approx.

827M
11¾" high

827L
14" high

827S
9¾" high

*749M
14½" high

7910M
9½" high
Made in crystal.
wheat & antique green

7048
19½" high
Boxed

8136S
15½" high

8136L
22½" high

8136M
18½" high

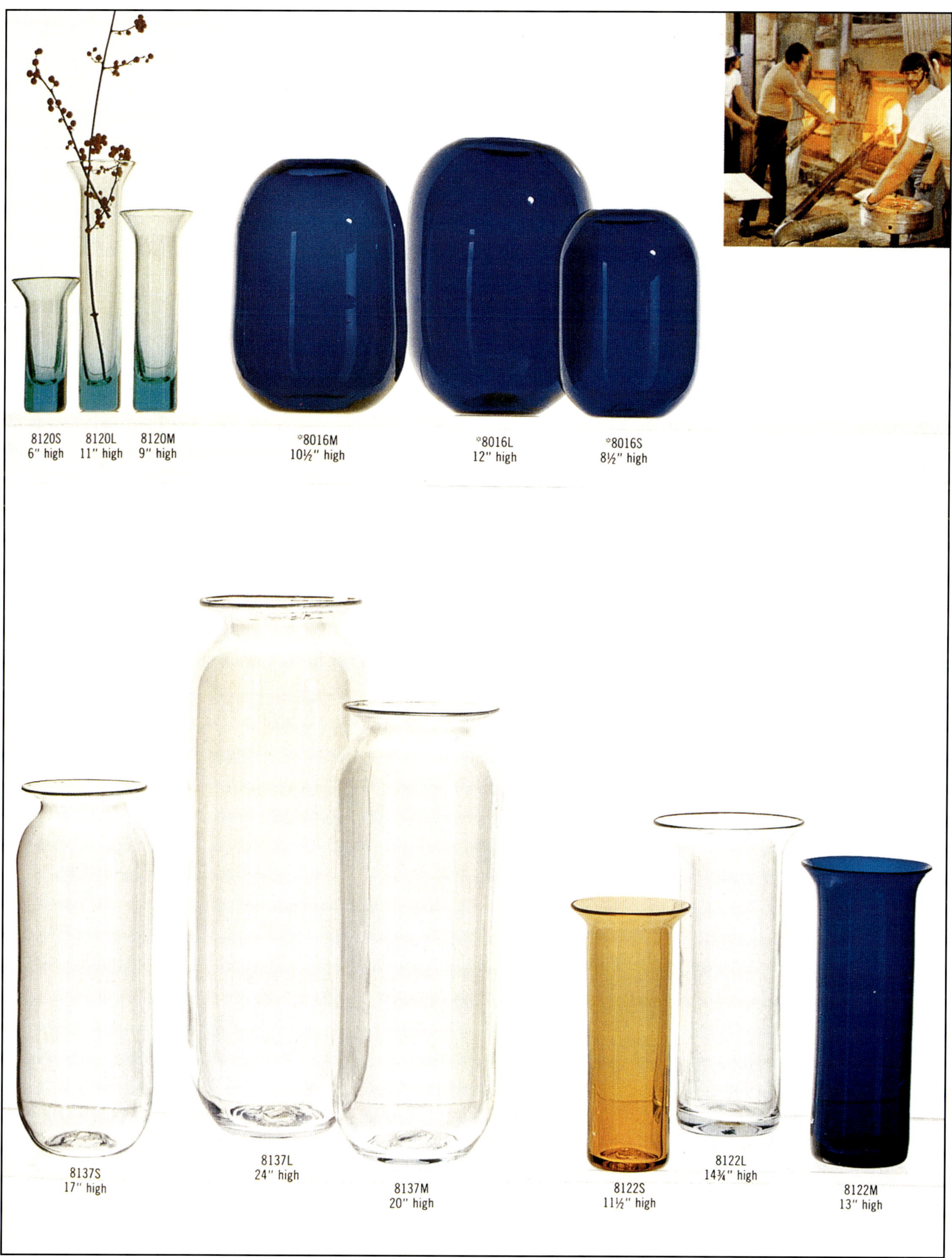

8120S 6" high 8120L 11" high 8120M 9" high

*8016M 10½" high

*8016L 12" high

*8016S 8½" high

8137S 17" high

8137L 24" high

8137M 20" high

8122S 11½" high

8122L 14¾" high

8122M 13" high

7818
6¼" high
*418S
4½" high
*418L
6" high
7911L
10" high
½ gal.
approx.
not made
in
sapphire
7911S
6" high
1 qt.
approx.
not made
in
sapphire
*745
6" high
*818L
9⅛" high
½ gal.
Approx.
*818S
6½" high
1 Qt.
approx.
7732
12⅜" dia.
Not made
in
sapphire
Specify crackled
top or plain
7918M
7½" high
*7116
6½" high
*3750L
5½" high
826S
11" high
Crystal
Only
826L
13" high
Crystal
Only
7922
7½" high approx
Not made in
Sapphire
706
6¾"
high
7029
16½" high
*64B
10" high
7738
16" high
not made in Sapphire
Please specify
Crackle top or plain

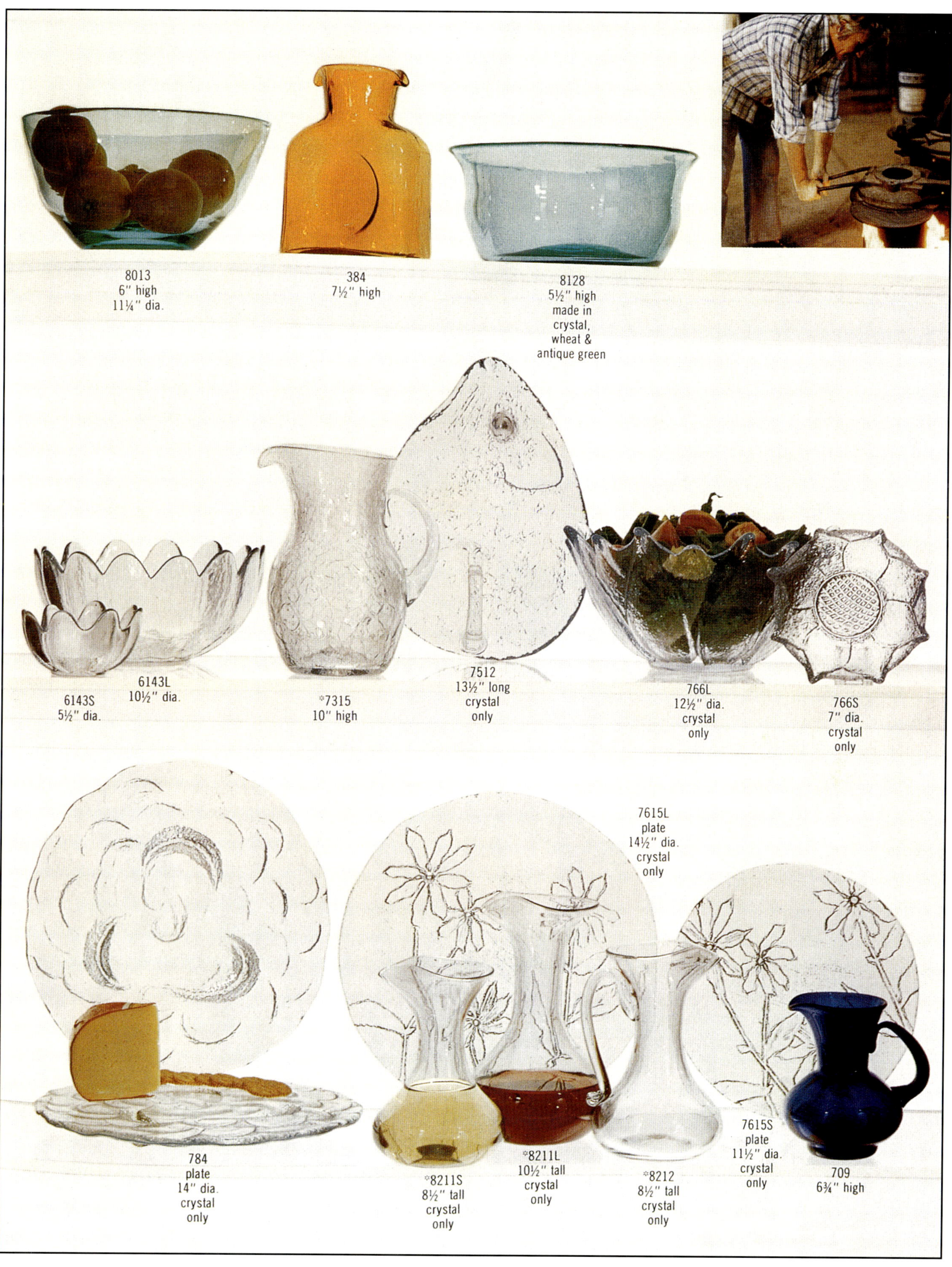

8013
6" high
11¼" dia.

384
7½" high

8128
5½" high
made in
crystal,
wheat &
antique green

6143S
5½" dia.

6143L
10½" dia.

*7315
10" high

7512
13½" long
crystal
only

766L
12½" dia.
crystal
only

766S
7" dia.
crystal
only

784
plate
14" dia.
crystal
only

7615L
plate
14½" dia.
crystal
only

*8211S
8½" tall
crystal
only

*8211L
10½" tall
crystal
only

*8212
8½" tall
crystal
only

7615S
plate
11½" dia.
crystal
only

709
6¾" high

7914
8" high
Not made
in
Sapphire
*8220
6⅝" high
8126
8" high
Not made
in
Sapphire
*990
12" high
990A
sold separately
990A
3⅛" dia
*6516
14½" high
8132M
11½" high
Crys. stoppers
only
7920
8½" high
*37
13" high
472
Mixed in box
or solid
59 crystals
mixed colors
only
*49
10½" high
829S
13" high
829L
15" high
8210
15" high
*6424
5" high
7727S
15" high
7728
15" high
789S
12¾" high

82A
Seashell
3⅝" dia.
approx.

82B
Seagull
3⅝" dia.
approx.

82C
Rooster
3⅝" dia.
approx.

82D
Black Eyed Susan
3⅝" dia. Approx.

82E
Daisy
3⅝" dia.
Approx.

82F
Dutch Flower
3⅝" dia. Approx.

821
Pencil Holder
4" tall Approx.

76A
6" high
approx.
Solid
crystal
or
Crystal/w/
green hat

76C
5¼" high approx.
Crystal only

76S
4" high approx.
Crystal only

76F
7" high approx.
Crystal only

76E
5½" high
Crystal only

76PG
3" high
Crystal only

823
7" x 4"
Solid crystal or
Crystal/w/wheat or Ant. green head
(please specify)

BLENKO
83

balloons
Blown up in glass, these festive pieces are the perfect containers for dried grasses and flowers.
Thumbing out bubble
828S
6¾" high
828L
11" high
828M
9¼" high
828S
6¾" high
828L
11" high
828M
9¼" high
The balloons are available in antique green/w/tangerine stripes only — sizes approximate . . .
826S
11" high
826L
13" high
8319
19¼" high
8323
14¼" high
8310M
15½" high
8310S
10" high

SNOW DRIFT

A rich subtle blend of opaque white and transparent blue with crystal glass . . . Projects the fresh beauty of a new snow—in the grouping of functional ware. Available only as shown.

The Batch House

8331L
5½" high

8332
7½" high

8330
ice bucket
8" high

8324
11" high

8328
9¼" high

8329
7½" high

8325
10¾" dia.
4¾" high

8327
10½" high

8326
10¼" high

8331L
5½" high

8331S
3⅝" high

Big Sky

Blue skies and green earth join with uniquely sculptured mountains to bring you this beautiful West Virginia "landscape" series of functional items. Also available in crystal.

Charging the Tank

8
12 8221L
12" high

8221S
9" high

8222
8" high

8225
12½" high

8224
7½" high

8227
ice bucket
9¼" high

8226
10¾" high

8223
4¾" high

8228
14" dia.
4½" high

Paddling the ball

*8314
6½" high

8120S
6" high

8120L
11" high

8120M
9" high

8320L
9¼" high

8320S
6¾" high

*8313
8" high

8328
9¼" high
as shown only

7728
15" high

829S
13" high

7048
19½" high
boxed

8317
9" high

Blowing

*7928S
7¾" high
approx.

*7928L
10¼" high
approx.

8121M
9" high

8121L
11" high

8121S
6" high

*8318
6¾" high
crystal with
blue rings
only

*8316
8½" high

*8016L
12" high

*8016M
10½" high

8137M
20" high

8321
12½" high

Finishing

*7315
10" high

8322L
9½" high

8322S
8¼" high

8315
9¾" dia.
6¼" high

*818L
9⅛" high
½ gal.
approx.

*818S
6½" high
1 qt.
approx.

7512
13½" long
crystal only

8013
11¼" dia.
6" high

6143L
10½" dia.

6143S
5½" dia.

7922
7½" high approx.
not made in
sapphire

*7116
6½" high

*3750L
5½" high

784
14" dia.
crystal only

Attaching the handle

Making a mold

8018
5" high

8312
10" high
crystal
stoppers
only

*37
13" high

*8220
6⅝" high

706
6¾" high

*6516
14½" high

8132M
11½" high
crys. stoppers
only

8017
9½" high

*49
10½" high

472
solid pack
or mixed

59
mixed
colors
only

7914
8" high
not made in
sapphire

8311S
9¼" high

8311L
14¾" high

8311M
11¼" high

*6424
5" high

7727S
15" high

*64B
10" high

829L
15" high

829S
13" high

8137L
24″ high

WHEAT

789L
25″ high

SAPPHIRE

7727L
28″ high
boxed

ANTIQUE GREEN

8310L
24¼″ high

CRYSTAL

Value Guide
Blenko Glass 1972-1983 Catalogs

The first two digits signify the year of introduction, except that the ones in the 90s were used in the early 1950s. The last digit(s) indicate the design order in that year. Prices are in U.S. dollars for single items, even if shown in pairs. Colorless (Crystal) items are generally at the low end of the value range or lower.

Abbreviations: S=small; M=medium; L=large; W/S=with stopper.

37	$50-60
3744X	$25-35
3750L	$30-40
384	$20-30
388	$40-50
418S	$15-20
418L	$15-20
434	$10-15
472	$15-20
49	$50-60
B508	$25-35
51S	$5-10
51M	$10-15
51L	$15-20
5433	$75-100
59	$10-15
6138W/S	$250-350
6143S	$10-15
6143L	$35-45
624	$15-20
629	$35-45
629S	$25-35
6212	$150-200
633	$35-45
636S	$45-55
6320	$20-25
6321	$20-25
64B	$25-35
64D	$25-35
6424	$25-35
65CP	$20-25
65GM	$20-25
65TR	$20-25
65LE	$20-25
65SG	$20-25
65VR	$20-25
65PS	$20-25
65CN	$20-25
65AR	$20-25
65SG	$20-25
65AQ	$20-25
65LB	$20-25
6511	$30-40
6516	$75-100
67S	$40-50
675	$25-30
6714	$35-45
6716	$150-200
6725	$20-30
6741	$200-250
68A	$30-40
68B	$30-40
68C	$30-40
68D	$35-45
68E	$30-40
68F	$40-50
68G	$30-40
68H	$35-45
681	$15-20
6810	$45-55
6811	$75-95
6813	$15-20
6840	$70-90
693	$10-15
694	$20-30
695	$15-20
697S	$20-25
697L	$30-40
698	$20-30
699A	$20-30
699B	$15-20
6914	$25-35
6916	$30-40
6918	$30-40
6919	$35-45
6928	$125-150
6934	$150-200
6937	$125-150
6942	$70-90
6944	$65-75
6950	$40-50
6951	$200-300
6952	$55-75
6953	$150-200
6954	$200-300
6955	$150-250
6956	$100-125
70	$10-15
701	$20-25
702	$15-20
703	$25-30
705	$20-25
706	$15-20
707	$20-25
708	$45-55
709	$20-30
7017	$20-25
7018	$70-90
7020S	$10-15
7020M	$15-20
7020L	$20-25
7028	$25-35
7029	$60-80
7033	$125-150
7048	$100-125
7049	$100-125
7051	$80-100
7054	$300-400
711A	$25-35
711B	$25-35
711C	$25-35
711F	$25-35
713	$40-50
715	$40-50
717	$70-90
719	$70-90
7111	$40-50
7112	$60-70
7114	$60-70
7115S	$25-35
7115M	$55-65
7115L	$75-125
7116	$30-40
7117	$30-40
7118	$150-200
7119	$70-90
7119W/S	$125-175
7120	$40-50

7121	$50-60
7122	$60-80
7125	$80-120
7126	$80-100
7127	$125-150
7128S	$25-35
7128L	$45-55
7129	$40-50
7137	$30-40
7141	$35-45
7143S	$30-40
7143M	$40-50
7143L	$50-70
7166M	$40-50
7166L	$55-65
721	$15-25
722S	$15-20
722M	$20-25
722L	$30-35
723	$10-15
724	$10-15
725A	$20-25
725B	$20-25
725C	$20-25
725D	$20-25
725E	$20-25
726	$20-30
727	$25-35
728	$25-35
729	$45-55
7210	$35-45
7211	$50-70
7212	$50-60
7213	$60-70
7213X	$200-250
7214S	$35-45
7214L	$55-65
7215SS	$50-70
7215L	$70-90
7216	$60-80
7217S	$20-30
7217L	$30-40
7218	$40-50
7219	$70-90
7220S	$70-90
7220L	$125-150
7221	$60-80
7221X	$200-300
7222	$150-200
7222X	$400-500
7223	$100-125
7224	$150-200
7225	$100-150
7225X	$300-400
7226S	$50-70
7226M	$80-100
7226L	$100-125
7227S	$25-35
7227M	$40-50
7227L	$55-65
7228S	$15-20
7228M	$15-20
7228L	$20-25
7228LL	$30-35
7229S	$60-80
7229L	$80-100
7230	$75-100
7231	$40-50
7231X	$200-250
7232	$50-70
7232X	$200-250
7233X	$200-250
7234X	$200-250
7235	$400-500
7236	$175-225
7237	$20-25
7238	$20-25
7239X	$300-400
7240X	$200-300
73S	$10-15
73L	$25-30
731	$20-25
732	$25-35
733	$35-45
734	$35-45
735	$20-25
736	$20-25
737	$10-15
738	$15-20
7310	$10-15
7311	$10-15
7312S	$25-35
7312L	$35-45
7313S	$25-35
7313L	$35-45
7314	$20-25
7315	$40-50
7316	$25-35
7317	$30-40
7318	$40-50
7319	$40-50
7320	$100-125
7321	$75-100
7322	$60-80
7323	$75-100
7324S	$10-15
7324L	$20-25
7325	$70-90
7326	$100-125
7327S	$60-80
7327L	$100-125
7328	$70-90
7329S	$15-20
7329L	$30-40
7330S	$20-30
7330M	$30-40
7330L	$40-50
7331	$60-80
7332	$50-70
7333	$15-20
7334	$150-250
7335	$100-150
74	$10-15
741	$15-20
742	$15-20
743	$15-20
744	$15-20
745	$20-25
746	$15-25
747	$25-35
748S	$10-15
748L	$15-25
749S	$25-35
749M	$45-55
749L	$65-75
7410	$35-45
7411	$70-90
7412	$75-100
7413	$100-125
7414	$90-120
7415	$75-100
7416	$100-125
7417	$25-35
7418	$50-60

7419	$35-45
7420	$30-40
7421	$20-25
7422	$30-40
7423	$50-60
7424	$40-50
7425S	$30-40
7425L	$40-50
7426S	$10-15
7426L	$20-25
7427	$35-45
7428S	$70-90
7428L	$100-125
7429	$70-90
7430	$125-175
7431	$125-175
7432	$300-400
751	$25-35
752	$10-15
753	$30-40
754	$30-40
755	$30-40
756	$15-20
757	$25-35
758	$25-35
759	$25-35
7510	$60-80
7511	$75-100
7512	$50-70
7513	$50-70
7514	$30-40
7515S	$40-50
7515L	$60-70
7516	$30-40
7517S	$20-30
7517L	$40-50
7518	$35-45
7519S	$40-50
7519L	$60-70
7520	$15-20
7521S	$75-100
7521L	$100-125
7522	$10-15
7523	$10-15
7524	$20-30
7525	$75-100
7526	$30-40
7527	$50-60
7528	$100-150
7529	$100-150
76A	$30-40
76B	$30-40
76C	$30-40
76D	$30-40
76E	$30-40
76F	$30-40
76G	$30-40
76K	$30-40
76S	$30-40
76W	$30-40
761	$10-15
762	$10-15
762G	$15-20
763	$20-30
764	$15-20
765	$10-15
766S	$10-15
766L	$20-30
767	$20-25
768	$35-45
769	$10-15
7610	$30-40
7611	$15-25
7612	$15-20
7613	$20-25
7614	$25-35
7615S	$20-25
7615L	$35-45
7616S	$25-35
7616L	$35-45
7617	$35-45
7618	$35-45
7619	$25-35
7620	$20-25
7622S	$40-50
7622L	$70-90
7623	$70-90
7624	$15-20
7626A	$25-35
7626B	$25-35
7626C	$25-35
7626D	$25-35
7627	$100-125
7628S	$30-40
7628L	$60-80
7629S	$15-20
7629L	$25-35
7630	$15-20
7631	$40-60
7632	$35-45
7633	$25-30
7634	$20-25
7635	$20-25
7636	$20-25
7637S	$20-25
7637L	$30-35
7638S	$20-25
7638L	$30-35
7639	$25-35
7640S	$60-80
7640M	$100-125
7640L	$150-250
7641S	$70-90
7641L	$150-200
7642	$70-90
7643	$50-60
7644	$100-150
7645	$100-125
77S	$10-15
77M	$10-15
77L	$10-15
771C	$10-15
771D	$8-10
771L	$15-20
771N	$8-10
771S	$8-10
772	$25-35
773	$45-65
772D	$15-20
772P	$10-15
773D	$25-35
773P	$20-30
774	$10-15
775	$15-20
776	$15-20
777	$15-20
778	$15-20
7710	$20-30
7711	$15-20
7712	$25-30
7713	$15-20
7714	$25-35
7716	$40-60
7717	$35-45
7718	$30-40
7719	$40-50
7720	$60-80
7721	$70-90
7722	$70-90
7723	$70-90
7724	$40-60
7724B	$10-15
7724G	$30-40

7725	$80-100
7726	$50-60
7727S	$100-125
7727L	$150-200
7728	$60-80
7729	$60-80
7730	$60-80
7731	$50-70
7732	$50-70
7733	$50-70
7734	$50-70
7735	$70-90
7736	$20-30
7737	$20-30
7738	$100-125
7739S	$60-80
7739L	$70-90
7740S	$30-50
7740L	$60-80
7741S	$20-30
7741M	$25-35
7741L	$35-45
78	$15-25
781	$15-20
782	$20-30
783	$20-25
784	$25-35
785	$15-25
786S	$30-40
786L	$40-50
787S	$10-15
787L	$15-20
788S	$20-30
789S	$60-80
789M	$80-100
789L	$125-150
7810	$30-40
7811	$25-35
7813	$15-20
7814	$20-30
7815	$10-15
7816	$10-15
7817	$30-40
7818	$30-40
7819	$40-50
7820	$30-40
7821	$20-30
7822	$30-40
7823	$35-45
7824	$30-40
7825	$60-80
7826	$20-30
7827	$30-40
7828	$40-50
7829	$10-15
7830	$10-20
7831	$15-25
7832	$15-20
7833	$20-30
7834	$50-70
7835	$25-35
7836	$60-80
7837	$15-25
7838	$35-45
7839	$20-30
791	$10-15
792	$10-15
793S	$30-40
793L	$40-60
794	$25-35
7910S	$10-15
7910M	$20-25
7910L	$30-40
7911S	$10-20
7911L	$20-30
7912S	$15-25
7912L	$25-35
7913	$20-30
7914	$25-35
7915S	$60-80
7915L	$100-125
7916	$35-45
7917	$60-80
7918S	$20-25
7918M	$40-50
7918L	$40-50
7919	$50-60
7921	$60-80
7922	$25-30
7923S	$50-60
7923M	$70-90
7923L	$100-125
7924	$100-200
7926S	$25-35
7926M	$25-35
7926L	$30-50
7927	$30-40
7928S	$50-60
7928M	$70-80
7928L	$100-125
7929	$25-35
801	$15-20
802S	$8-10
802M	$10-15
802L	$15-20
803	$10-15
804S	$10-15
804L	$20-25
805	$5-10
806S	$20-30
806M	$30-40
806L	$50-70
807	$10-15
808	$15-20
809	$50-70
8010	$40-50
8011	$20-25
8012	$25-35
8013	$25-35
8014	$60-80
8015S	$40-50
8015M	$50-60
8015L	$80-100
8016S	$30-40
8016M	$40-50
8016L	$50-70
8017	$50-60
8018	$20-30
8019S	$50-60
8019L	$70-90
8020S	$60-80
8020L	$100-150
8021	$60-80
8022	$100-200
8023	$100-200
8024	$100-200
8026	$30-40
8027	$10-20
810	$10-15
81A	$30-40
81B	$30-40
811	$15-25
812	$20-25
813	$15-25
814	$30-40
815	$25-35
816	$25-35
817	$25-35
818S	$15-20
818L	$25-30
8118	$15-25
8120S	$15-25
8120M	$25-35

8120L	$35-45
8121S	$15-25
8121M	$25-35
8121L	$35-45
8122S	$35-45
8122M	$45-55
8122L	$55-65
8123	$20-30
8124S	$20-25
8124M	$35-45
8124L	$50-70
8125S	$30-40
8125L	$40-50
8126	$25-35
8127	$25-35
8128	$30-40
8129	$30-40
8130S	$25-35
8130L	$35-45
8131S	$25-35
8131L	$50-70
8132M	$70-90
8132L	$125-150
8133	$30-40
8134S	$100-150
8134M	$150-250
8134L	$250-350
8135S	$40-50
8135M	$60-70
8135L	$80-100
8136S	$60-80
8136M	$70-90
8136L	$100-150
8137S	$40-50
8137M	$60-70
8137L	$80-100
8138	$50-70
8139	$125-225
8140	$15-20
82A	$20-30
82B	$20-30
82C	$20-30
82D	$20-30
82E	$20-30
82F	$20-30
821	$15-25
822	$15-20
823	$30-50
824	$10-15
825	$15-20
826S	$50-60
826L	$70-90
827S	$30-40
827M	$40-50
827L	$50-60
828S	$60-80
828M	$100-125
828L	$150-200
829S	$40-50
829L	$50-60
8210	$50-60
8211S	$20-30
8211L	$35-45
8212	$30-40
8213	$30-40
8214	$15-20
8216S	$30-40
8216M	$50-60
8216L	$80-100
8217M	$50-60
8217L	$80-100
8219S	$50-60
8219L	$50-60
8221S	$50-70
8221L	$70-90
8222	$30-50
8223	$30-50
8224	$30-50
8225	$70-90
8227	$60-80
8228	$60-80
831	$30-40
833	$30-40
834	$10-15
835	$10-20
836	$15-20
837	$15-25
838S	$10-15
838L	$20-25
839	$10-20
8310S	$30-40
8310M	$50-70
8310L	$80-100
8311S	$20-25
8311M	$30-35
8311L	$40-45
8312	$50-60
8313	$20-25
8314	$20-25
8315	$25-35
8316	$25-35
8317	$20-25
8318	$30-40
8319	$100-150
8320S	$20-25
8320L	$30-40
8321	$25-35
8322S	$25-35
8322L	$30-40
8323	$50-60
8324	$60-80
8325	$50-60
8326	$50-70
8327	$50-70
8328	$50-60
8329	$40-50
8330	$60-80
8331S	$20-25
8331L	$20-25
8332	$60-80
966	$20-30
971M	$70-80
971L	$100-150
990	$30-40
990A	$10-15
990B	$10-15
991	$60-70